MAD SH

L. P. Jacks

MAD SHEPHERDS

And Other Human Studies

Oxford   New York   Toronto   Melbourne
OXFORD UNIVERSITY PRESS
1979

Oxford University Press, Walton Street, Oxford OX2 6DP

OXFORD   LONDON   GLASGOW
NEW YORK   TORONTO   MELBOURNE   WELLINGTON
KUALA LUMPUR   SINGAPORE   JAKARTA   HONG KONG   TOKYO
DELHI   BOMBAY   CALCUTTA   MADRAS   KARACHI
NAIROBI   DAR ES SALAAM   CAPE TOWN

First published by Williams and Norgate 1910
First published as an Oxford University Press paperback
1979 at the suggestion of R. H. Hardy

British Library Cataloguing in Publication Data

Jacks, Lawrence Pearsall
Mad shepherds and other human studies.
I. Title
823'.9'1FS   PZ7.J/   79–40061

ISBN   0–19–281282–3

Set, printed and bound in Great Britain by
Cox & Wyman Ltd, Reading

CONTENTS

THERE is nothing that so embases and enthralls the Souls of men, as the dismall and dreadfull thoughts of their own Mortality, which will not suffer them to look beyond this short span of Time, to see an houres length before them, or to look higher than these materiall Heavens; which though they could be stretch'd forth to infinity, yet would the space be too narrow for an enlightned mind, that will not be confined within the compass of corporeal dimensions. These black Opinions of Death and the Non-entity of Souls (darker than Hell it self) shrink up the free-born Spirit which is within us, which would otherwise be dilating and spreading it self boundlessly beyond all Finite Being: and when these sorry pinching mists are once blown away, it finds this narrow sphear of Being to give way before it; and having once seen beyond Time and Matter, it finds then no more ends nor bounds to stop its swift and restless motion. It may then fly upwards from one heaven to another, till it be beyond all orbe of Finite Being, swallowed up in the boundless Abyss of Divinity, ὑπεράνω τῆς οὐσίας, beyond all that which darker thoughts are wont to represent under the Idea of Essence. This is that ἴκσο αντεόο which the Areopagite speaks of, which the higher our Minds soare into, the more incomprehensible they find it. Those dismall apprehensions which pinion the Souls of men to mortality, churlishly check and starve that noble life thereof, which would alwaies be rising upwards, and spread it self in a free heaven: and when once the Soul hath shaken off these, when it is once able to look through a grave, and see beyond death, it finds a vast Immensity of Being opening it self more and more before it, and the ineffable light and beauty thereof shining more and more into it.

Select Discourses of John Smith, the
Cambridge Platonist, 1660.

Mad Shepherds

*

SHOEMAKER HANKIN

AMONG the four hundred human beings who peopled our parish there were two notable men and one highly gifted woman. All three are dead, and lie buried in the churchyard of the village where they lived. Their graves form a group—unsung by any poet, but worthy to be counted among the resting-places of the mighty.

The woman was Mrs Abel, the Rector's wife. None of us knew her origin—I doubt if she knew it herself: beyond her husband and children, assignable relative she had none.

> 'Sie war nicht in dem Tal geboren,
> Man wusste nicht woher sie kam.'

Her husband met her many years ago at a foreign watering-place, and married her there after a week's acquaintance—much to the scandal of his family, for the lady was an actress not unknown to fame. Their only consolation was that she had a considerable fortune—the fruit of her professional work.

In all relevant particulars this strange venture had proved a huge success. To leave the fever of the stage for the quiet life of the village had been to Mrs Abel like the escape of a soul from the flames of purgatory. She had rightly discerned that the Rev. Edward Abel was a man of large heart, high character, and excellent wit—partly clergyman, but mostly man. He, on his part, valued his wife, and his judgment was backed by every humble soul in the village. But the bigwigs of the county, and every clergyman's wife within a radius of ten miles, were of another mind. She had not been 'proper' to begin with—at least, they said so; and as time went on she took no pains to be more 'proper' than she was at first. Her improprieties, so far as I could ever learn, arose from nothing more heinous than her possession of an intelligence more powerful and a courage more daring than that to which any of her neighbours could lay claim. Her outspokenness was a stumbling-block to many; and the offence of speaking her mind was aggravated by the circumstance, not always present at such times, that she had a mind to speak. To quote the language in which Farmer Perryman once explained the situation to me: 'She'd given all on 'em a taste o' the whip, and with some on 'em she'd peppered and salted the sore place into the bargain.' Moreover, she sided with many things that a clergyman's wife ought to oppose: took all sorts of undesirables under her protection, helped those whom everybody else wanted to punish, threw good discretion to the winds, and sometimes mixed in undertakings which no 'lady' ought to touch. To all this she added the impertinence of regular attendance at church, where she recited the Creeds in a rich voice that almost drowned her husband's, turning punctually to the East and bowing at the Sacred Name. That she was a hypocrite trying to save her face was, of course, obvious to every Scribe and Pharisee in the county. But the poor of Deadborough preferred her hypocrisy to the virtuous simplicity of her critics.

Mrs Abel is too great a subject for such humble portraiture as I can attempt, and she will henceforth appear in these pages only as occasion requires. It is time that we turn to the men.

The first of these was Robert Dellanow, known far and wide as 'Snarley Bob', head shepherd to Sam Perryman of the Upper Farm. I say, the first; for it was he who had the pre-eminence, both as to intelligence and the tragic antagonisms of his life. The man had many singularities, singular at least in shepherds. Perhaps the chief of these was the violence of the affinities and repulsions that broke forth from him towards every personality with whom he came into any, even the slightest, contact. Snarley invariably loved or hated at first sight, or rather at first sound, for he was strangely sensitive to the tones of a human voice. If, as seldom happened, your voice and presence chanced to strike the responsive chord, Snarley became your devoted slave on the spot; the heavy, even brutal, expression that his face often wore passed off like a cloud; you were in the Mount of Transfiguration, and it seemed that Elijah or one of the prophets had come back to earth. If, as was more likely, your manner repelled him, he would show signs of immediate distress; the animality of his features would become more sinister and forbidding; and if, undaunted by the first repulse, you continued to press your attentions upon him, he would presently break out into an ungovernable paroxysm of rage, accompanied by startling language and even by threats of violence, which drove offenders headlong from his presence. In these outbursts he was unrestrained by rank, age, or sex—indeed, his antipathies to certain women were the most violent of all. Curiously enough, it was the presence of humanity of the uncongenial type which alone had power to effect his reversion to the status of the brute. His normal condition was gentle and serene: he was fond of children and certain animals, and he bore the agonies of his old rheumatic limbs without a murmur of complaint.

It was not possible, of course, that such a man, however gifted with intelligence, should 'succeed in life'. There were some people who held that he was mad, and proposed that he should be put under restraint; and doubtless they would have gained their end had not Snarley been able to give proofs of his sanity in certain directions such as few men could produce.

Once he had been haled before the magistrate to answer a serious charge of using threats, was fined and compelled to give security for his good behaviour; and it was on this occasion that he narrowly escaped detention as a lunatic. Indeed, I cannot prove that he was sane; but neither could I prove it, if challenged, in regard to myself—a difficulty which the courteous reader, in his own case, will hardly deny that he has to share with me. Mad or sane, it is certain that Snarley, under a kinder Fate, might have been something more splendid than he was. Mystic, star-gazer, dabbler in black or blackish arts, he seemed in his lowly occupation of shepherd to represent some strange miscarriage of Nature's designs; but Mrs Abel, who understood the secrets of many hearts, always maintained that Snarley, the breeder of the famous Perryman rams, had found the calling to which he had been fore-ordained from the foundation of the world. Of this the reader must judge from the sequel; for we shall hear much of him anon.

The second man was Tom Hankin, shoemaker. A man of strong contrasts was Tom; an octogenarian when I first knew him, and an atheist, as he proudly boasted, 'all his life'. My last interview with him took place a few days before his death, when he knew that he was hovering on the brink of the grave; and it was then that Hankin offered me his complete argument for the non-existence of Deity and the mortality of the soul. Never did dying saint dilate on the raptures of Paradise with greater fervour than that displayed by the old man as he developed his theme. I will not say that Hankin was happy; but he was fierce and unconquered, and totally unafraid. I think also that he was proud—proud, that is, of his ability to hurl defiance into the very teeth of Death. He said that he had always hoped he would be able to die thus; that he had sometimes feared lest in his last illness there should be some weakening towards the end: perhaps his mind would become overclouded, and he would lose grip of his arguments; perhaps he would think that death was *something* instead of being *nothing*; perhaps he would be troubled by the thought of impending annihilation. But no, it was all as clear as before, clearer if anything. All that troubled him was 'that folks was so blind; that Snarley Bob, in particular, was as obstinate as ever—a man, sir, as ought to ha' known better; never would listen to no arguments; always shut him up when he tried to reason, and sometimes swore at him; and him with the best head in the whole county, but crammed full of rubbish that was no use to himself nor nobody else, and that nobody could make head nor tail of—no, not even Mrs Abel, as was always backing him up; and to think of him breedin' sheep all his life; why, that man, sir, if only he'd learned a bit o' common-sense reasonin', might ha' done wonders, instead o' wastin' himself

wi' a lot o' tomfoolery about stars and spirits, and what all.'
Thus he continued to pour forth till a fit of coughing interrupted the torrent.

Hankin was the son of a Chartist, from whom he inherited a
small but sufficient collection of books. Tom Paine was there, of
course, bearing on every page of him the marks of two generations of Hankin thumbs. He also possessed the works of John
Stuart Mill, not excepting the *Logic*, which he had mastered,
even as to the abstruser portions, with a thoroughness such as
few professors of the science could boast at the present day.
Mill, indeed, was his prophet; and the principle of the Greatest
Happiness was his guiding star. Hankin was well abreast of
current political questions, and to every one of them he applied
his principle and managed by means of it to take a definite side.
As he worked at his last he would concentrate his mind on
some chosen problem of social reform, and would ponder, with
singular pertinacity, the ways and degrees in which alternative
solutions of it would affect the happiness of men. He would
sometimes spend weeks in meditating thus on a single problem,
and, when a solution had been reached according to his
method, he made it a regular practice to go down to the Nag's
Head and announce the result, with all the prolixity of its ante-
cedents, over a pot of beer. It was there that I heard Hankin
defend 'armaments' as conducive to the Greatest Happiness of
the Greatest Number. Venturing to assail what I thought a
preposterous view, I was met by a counter attack of horse, foot,
and artillery, so well planned and vigorously sustained that in
the end I was utterly beaten from the field. Had Snarley Bob
been present, the result would have been different; indeed,
there would have been no result to the controversy at all. He
would have stopped the argument *ab initio* by affirming in
language of his own, perhaps unprintable, that the whole question was of not the slightest importance to anybody; that 'them
as built the ships, because someone had argued 'em into doing
it, were fools, and them as did the arguing were bigger fools
still'; the same for those who refrained from building; that, in
short, the only way to get such questions settled was 'to leave

'em to them as knows what's what'. This ignorant and undemocratic attitude never failed to divert Hankin from argument to recrimination, which was all the more bitter because Bob had a way of implying, mainly by the movement of his horse-like eyes, that he himself was one of those who knew precisely what 'what' was. The upshot therefore was a row between shepherd and shoemaker—a thing which the shepherd enjoyed in the same degree as he hated the shoemaker's arguments.

Not the least of Mrs Abel's improprieties was her open patronage of Hankin. The shoemaker had established what he called an Ethical Society, which held its meetings on Sunday afternoons in the barn of a sympathetic farmer. These meetings, which were regularly addressed by Hankin, Mrs Abel used frequently to attend. The effect of this was twofold. On the one hand, it was no small stimulus to Hankin that among the handful of uneducated irreconcilables who gathered to hear him, he might have for auditor one of the keenest and most cultivated minds in England—one who, as he was well aware, had no sympathy with his opinions. I once heard him lecture on one of his favourite topics while she was present, and I must say that I have seldom heard a bad case better argued. On the other hand, Mrs Abel's presence served to rob his lectures of much of the force which opinions, when condemned by the rich, invariably have among the poor. She was shrewd enough to perceive that active repression of Hankin, who she well knew could not be repressed, would only swell his following and strengthen his position.

This, of course, was not understood by the local guardians of morality and religion. After vainly appealing to Mr Abel, who turned an absolutely deaf ear to the petitioners, they proceeded to lay the case before the Bishop, who happened to be, unfortunately for them, one of the most courageous and enlightened prelates of his time. The Bishop, on whom considerable pressure was brought to bear, resolved at last to come down to Deadborough and have an interview with Mrs Abel. The result was that he and the lady became fast and lifelong friends. He returned to his palace determined to take the risk, and to all further importunities he merely returned a formal answer that he saw no reason to interfere. This was not the least daring of many actions which have distinguished, by their boldness and commonsense, the record of a singularly noble career. The case did not get into the papers; none the less, it was much talked of in clerical circles, and its effect was to give the Bishop a reputation among prelates not unlike that which Mrs Abel had won among clergymen's wives.

The Bishop's intervention having failed, the party of repression now determined on the short and easy way. Hankin's landlord was Peter Shott, whose holding consisted of two small farms which had been joined together. In the house belonging to one of these farms lived Hankin, a sub-tenant of Shott. To Shott there came, in due course, a hint from an exalted quarter that it would be to his interests to give Hankin notice to quit. Shott was willing enough, and presently the notice was served. It was a serious thing for the shoemaker, for he had a good business, and there was no other house or cottage available in the neighbourhood.

In the interval before the notice expired announcements appeared that the estate to which Shott's holding belonged was to be sold by auction in lots. Shott himself was well-to-do, and promptly determined to become the purchaser of his farm.

There were several bidders at the sale, and Shott was pushed to the very end of his tether. He managed, however, to outbid them all, though he trembled at his own temerity; and the farm was on the point of being knocked down to him when a lawyer's clerk at the end of the room went £50 better. Shott took a gulp of whisky to steady his nerve and desperately put the price up fifty more. The lawyer's clerk immediately countered with another hundred, and looked as though he was ready to go on. That was the knock-down blow. Shott put his hands in his pockets, leaned back in his chair, and dolefully shook his head in response to all the coaxings and blandishments of the auctioneer. The hammer fell. 'Name, please,' was called; the lawyer's clerk passed up a slip of paper, and a thunderbolt fell on the company when the auctioneer read out,

'Mr Thomas Hankin.' Hankin had bought the farms for £4700. 'Cheque for deposit,' said the auctioneer. A cheque for £470, previously signed by Hankin, was immediately filled in and passed up by the lawyer's clerk.

It was, of course, Mrs Abel who had advanced the money to the shoemaker on prospective mortgage, less a sum of £1000 which he himself contributed—the savings of his life. The situation became interesting. Here was Hankin, under notice to quit, now become the rightful owner of his own house and the landlord of his landlord. Everyone read what had happened as a deep-laid scheme of vengeance on the part of Hankin and Mrs Abel, of whose part in the transaction no secret whatever was made. It was taken for granted that the evicted man would now retaliate by turning Shott out of his highly cultivated farm and well-appointed house. The jokers of the Nag's Head were delirious, and drank gin in their beer for a week after the occurrence. Snarley Bob alone drank no gin, and merely contributed the remark that 'them as laughs last, laughs best'.

Meanwhile the shoemaker, seated at his last, was carefully pondering the position in the light of the principles of Bentham and Mill. He considered all the possible alternatives and weighed off against one another the various amounts of pleasure and pain involved, resolutely counting himself as 'one and not more than one'. He certainly estimated at a large figure the amount of pleasure he himself would derive from paying Shott in his own coin. All consideration of 'quality' was strictly eliminated, for in this matter Hankin held rather with Bentham than with Mill. The sum was an extremely complicated one to work, and gave more exercise to Hankin's powers of moral arithmetic than either armaments, or women's suffrage, or the State Church. Mrs Abel had left him free to do exactly as he liked; and he had nearly determined to expel Shott when it occurred to him that by taking the other course he would give a considerable amount of pleasure to the Rector's wife. And to this must be added the pleasure which he would derive for himself by pleasing her, and further the pleasure of his chief friend and enemy, Snarley Bob, on discovering that both of them were pleased. Then there was the question of his own reflected pleasure in the pleasure of Snarley Bob, and this was considerable also; for though Hankin denounced Bob on every possible occasion, yet secretly he valued his good opinion more than that of any living man. It is true that the figures at which he estimated these personal quantities were very small in proportion to those which he had set down to the more public aspects of the case; for his principles forbade him to reckon either Mrs Abel or Snarley as 'more than one'. Nevertheless, small as these figures were, Hankin found, when he came to add up his totals and strike off the balance of pains, that they were enough to turn the scale. He determined to leave Shott undisturbed, and went to bed with that feeling of perfect mental satisfaction which did duty with him for a conscience at peace.

Notice of this resolution was conveyed next day to the parties concerned, and that night Farmer Shott, who was a pious Methodist and held family prayers, instead of imploring the Almighty 'to defeat the wiles of Satan, now active in this village', put up a lengthy petition for blessings on the heads of Shoemaker Hankin and his family, mentioning each one of them by name, and adding such particulars of his or her special needs as would leave the Divine Benevolence with no excuse for mixing them up.

With all his hard-headedness Hankin combined the graces of a singularly kind and tender heart. He held, of course, that there was nothing like leather, especially for mitigating the distress of the orphan and causing the widow's heart to sing for joy. Every year he received confidentially from the schoolmistress a list of the worst-shod children in the school, from whom he selected a dozen belonging to the poorest families, that he might provide each of them at Christmas with a pair of good, strong shoes. The boots of labourers out of work and of other unfortunates he mended free of cost, regularly devoting to this purpose that part of the Sabbath which was not occupied in proving the non-existence of God. There was, for instance, poor Mary Henson—a loose, deserted creature with illegitimate

children of various paternity, and another always on the
way—rejected by every charity in the parish,—to whom Hankin
never failed to send needed footwear both for herself and her
brats.

Further, whenever a pair of shoes had to be condemned as
'not worth mending', he endeavoured to retain them for a purpose of his own, sometimes paying a few pence for them as 'old
leather'. When summer came round he set to work patching
the derelicts as best he could, and would sometimes have thirty
or forty pairs in readiness by the end of June. This was the
season when the neighbourhood was annually invaded by
troops of pea-pickers—a very miscellaneous collection of humanity, comprising at the one extreme broken army men and
university graduates, and at the other the lowest riff-raff of the
towns. It was Hankin's regular custom to visit the camps where
these people were quartered, with the avowed object of 'study-
ing human nature', but really for the purpose of spying out the
shoeless, or worse than shoeless, feet. He was a notable per-
former on the concertina, and I well remember seeing him in
the middle of a pea-field, surrounded by as sorry a group of
human wreckage as civilization could produce, listening, or
dancing to his strains. Hankin's eyes were on their feet all the
time. When the performance was over he went round to one
and another, mostly women, and said something which made
their eyes glisten.

And here it may be recorded that one day, towards the end of
his life, he received a letter from Canada containing a remit-
tance for fifty pounds. The writer, Major —— of the North-
West Mounted Police, said that the money was payment for a
certain pair of old shoes, the gift of which 'had set him on his
feet in more senses than one'. He also stated that he had made
a small fortune by speculating in town-lots, and, hearing that
Hankin was alive, he was prepared to send him any further
sum of money that might be necessary to secure him a comfortable old age. Major —— died last year, and left by his will the
sum of £300 in Consols to the Rector and churchwardens of
Deadborough, the interest to be expended annually at Christ-

mas in providing boots and shoes for the poor of the parish.

In the matter of trade Hankin was prosperous, and fully deserved his prosperity. He has been dead four years, and I am wearing at this moment almost the last pair of boots he ever made. His materials were the best that could be procured, and his workmanship was admirable. His customers were largely the well-to-do people of the neighbourhood, and his standard price for walking-boots was thirty-three shillings. He was by no means incapable of the higher refinements of 'style', so that great people like Lady Passingham or Captain Sorley were often heard to say that they preferred his goods to those of Bond Street. He did a large business in building shooting-boots for the numerous parties which gathered at Deadborough Hall; his customers recommended him in the London clubs, where such things are talked of, and he received orders from all parts of the country and at all times of the year. He might, no doubt, have made his fortune. But he would have no assistance save that of his two sons. He lived for thirty-seven years in the house from which Shott had sought to expel him, refusing all orders which exceeded the limited working forces at his command. He charted the corns on many noble feet; he measured the gouty toe of a Duke to the fraction of a millimetre, and made a contour map of all its elevations from the main peak to the foot-hills; and it was said that a still more Exalted Personage occasionally walked on leather of his providing.

Hankin neglected nothing which might contribute to the success of his work, and applied himself to its principles with the same thoroughness which distinguished his handling of the Utilitarian Standard. One of his sons had emigrated to the United States and become, in course of time, the manager of a large boot factory in Brockton, Mass. From him Hankin received patterns and lasts and occasional consignments of American leather. This latter he was inclined, in general, to despise. Nevertheless, it had its uses. He found that an outer sole of hemlock-tanned leather would greatly lengthen the working life of a poor man's heavy boot; though for want of suppleness it was useless for goods supplied to the 'quality'. The

American patterns and lasts, on the other hand, he treated with great respect. He held that they embodied a far sounder knowledge of the human foot than did the English variety, and found them a great help to his trade in giving style, comfort, and accuracy of fit. At a time when the great manufacturers of Stafford and Northampton were blundering along with a range of four or five standard patterns, Hankin, in his little shop, was working on much finer intervals and producing nine regular sizes of men's boots. Indeed, his ready-made goods were so excellent, and their 'fit' so certain, that some of his customers preferred them, and ordered him to abandon their lasts.

Such was Hankin's manner of life and conversation. If there is such a place as heaven, and the reader ever succeeds in getting there, let him look out for Shoemaker Hankin among the highest seats of glory. His funeral oration was pronounced, though not in public, by Snarley Bob. 'Shoemaker Hankin were a great man. He'd got hold o' lots o' good things; but he'd got some on 'em by the wrong end. He *talked* more than a man o' his size ought to ha' done. He spent his breath in proving that God doesn't exist, and his life in proving that He does.'

SNARLEY BOB ON THE STARS

Towards the end of his life there were few persons with whom Snarley would hold converse, for his contempt of the human race was immeasurable. There was Mrs Abel at the Rectory, whom he adored; there were the Perrymans, whom he loved; and there was myself, whom he tolerated. There was also his old wife, whom he treated as part of himself, neither better nor worse. With other human beings—saving only the children—his intercourse was limited as far as possible to interjectory grunts and snarls—whence his name.

It was in an old quarry among the western hills, on a bleak January day not long before his death, that I met Snarley Bob and heard him discourse of the everlasting stars. The quarry was the place in which to find Snarley most at his ease. In the little room of his cottage he could hardly be persuaded to speak; the confined space made him restless; and, as often as not, if a question were asked him he would seem not to hear it, and would presently get up, walk out of the door, and return when it pleased him. 'He do be growing terrible absent-minded,' his wife would often say in these latter days. 'I'm a'most afraid sometimes as he may be took in a fit.' But in the old quarry he was another man. The open spaces of the sky seemed to bring him to himself.

Many a time on a summer day I have watched Mrs Abel's horse bearing its rider up the steep slope that led to the quarry, and more than once have I gone thither myself only to find that she had forestalled my hopes of an interview. 'Snarley Bob,' she used to say to me, with a frank disregard for my own feelings—'Snarley Bob is the one man in the world whom I have found worth talking to.'

The feature in Snarley's appearance that no one could fail to see, or, having seen, forget, was the extraordinary width between the eyes. It was commonly said that he had the power of seeing people behind his back. And so doubtless he had, but the thing was no miracle. It was a consequence of the position of his eyes, which, like those of a horse, were as much at the side of his head as they were in front.

Snarley's manner of speech was peculiar. Hoarse and hesitating at first, as though the physical act were difficult, and rising now and then into the characteristic snarl, his voice would presently sink into a deep and resonant note and flow freely onward in a tone of subdued emphasis that was exceedingly impressive. Holding, as he did, that words are among the least important things of life, Snarley was nevertheless the master of an unforced manner of utterance more convincing by its quiet indifference to effect than all the preternatural pomposities of the pulpit and the high-pitched logic of the schools. I have often thought that any Cause or Doctrine which could get itself expressed in Snarley's tones would be in a fair way to conquer the world. Fortunately for the world, however, it is not every Cause, nor every Doctrine, which would lend itself to expression in that manner.

Seated on a heap of broken road metal, with a doubled sack between his person and the stones, and with his short pipe stuck out at right angles to his profile, so that he could see what was going on in the bowl, Snarley Bob discoursed, at intervals, as follows:

'Yes, sir, there's things about the stars that fair knocks you silly to think on. And, what's more, you can't think on 'em, leastways to no good purpose, until they *have* knocked you silly. Why, what's the good of tellin' a man that it's ninety-three millions o' miles between the earth and the sun? There's lots o' folks as knows that; but there's not one in ten thousand as knows what it means. You gets no forrader wi' lookin' at the figures in a book. You must thin yourself out, and make your body lighter than air, and stretch and stretch at yourself until you gets the sun and planets, floatin' like, in the middle o' your mind. Then you begins to get hold on it. Or what's the good o' sayin' that Saturn has rings and nine moons? You must go to one o' them moons, and see Saturn fillin' half the sky, wi' his rings cuttin' the heavens from top to bottom, all coloured wi' crimson and gold—then you begins to stagger at it. That's why I say you can't think o' these things till they've knocked you silly. Now there's Sir Robert Ball—it's knocked him silly, I can tell you. I knowed that when I went to his lecture, by the pictures he showed us, and I sez to myself, "Bob", I sez, "that's a man worth listenin' to".

'You're right, sir. I wouldn't pay the least attention to anything you might say about the stars unless you'd told me that it knocked you silly to think on 'em. No, and I wouldn't talk to you about 'em either. You wouldn't understand.

'And, as you were sayin', it isn't easy to get them big things the right way up. When things get beyond a certain bigness you don't know which way up they are; and as like as not they're standin' on their heads when you think they're standin' on their heels. That's the way with the stars. They all want lookin' at t'other way up from what most people looks at 'em. And perhaps it's a good thing they looks at 'em the wrong way; becos if they looked at 'em the right way it would scare 'em out o' their wits, especially the women—same as it does my missis when she hears me and Mrs Abel talkin'. Always exceptin' Mrs Abel; you can't scare her; and she sees most things right way up, that she does!

'But when it comes to the stars, you want to be a bit of a *medium* before you can get at 'em. Oh yes, I've been a medium in my time, more than I care to think of, and I could be a medium again to-morrow, if I wanted to. But them's the only sort of folks as can see things from both ends. Most folks only looks at things from one end—and that as often as not the wrong un. Mediums looks from both ends; and, if they're good at it, they soon finds out which end's right. You see, some on 'em—like me, for instance—can throw 'emselves out o' 'emselves, in a manner o' speaking, so that they can see their own bodies, just as if they was miles away, same as I can see that man walking on the Deadborough Road.

'Well, I've often done it, and many's the story I could tell of things I've seen by day and night; but it wasn't till I went to hear Sir Robert Ball as the grand idea came to me. "Why not throw yerself into the stars, Bob?" I sez to myself. And, by gum, sir, I did it that very night. How I did it I don't know; I won't say as there weren't a drop o' drink in it; but the minute I'd *got through,* I felt as I'd stretched out wonderful, and blessed if I didn't find myself standin' wi' millions of other spirits, right in the middle o' Saturn's rings. And the things I see there I couldn't tell you, no, not if you was to give me a thousand pounds. Talk o' spirits! I tell you there was millions on 'em! And the lights and the colours—oh, but it's no good talkin'! I looked back and wanted to know where the earth was, and there I see it, dwindled to a speck o' light.

'Now you can understand why I keeps my mouth shut. Do you think I'm going to talk of them things to a lot o' folks that's got no more sense nor swine? Not me! And what else is there that's worth talking on? Who's goin' to make a fuss and go blatherin' about this and that, when you know the whole earth's no bigger nor a pea? My eyes! if some o' these 'ere talkin' politicians knowed half o' what I know, they'd stop their blowin' pretty quick.

'There's our parson—and he's a good man, though not half good enough for *her*—why, you might as well talk to a babby three months old! If I told him, he'd only think I was crazy; and like as not he'd send for old Doctor Kenyon to come up and feel my head, same as they did wi' Shepherd Toller, Clun Downs way, before they put him in the asylum. I sometimes says to my missis that it's a good thing I'm a poor man wi' nowt but a flock o' sheep to look after. For don't you see, sir, when once you've got hold o' the bigness o' things it's all one—flocks o' sheep and nations o' men? If I were King o' England, or Prime Minister, or any sort o' great man, knowing what I know, I'd only think I were a bigger humbug nor the rest. I couldn't keep it up. But bein' only a shepherd, I've got nothing to keep up, and I'm thankful I haven't.

'I allus knows when folks has got things wrong end up by the amount they talks. When you get 'em the right way you don't *want* to talk on 'em, except it may be to one or two, like Mrs Abel, as got 'em the same way as yourself. So when you hears folks jawin', you can allers tell what's the matter wi' 'em.

'There's old Shoemaker Hankin at Deadborough. Know him? Well, did you ever hear such a blatherin' old fool? "All these things you're mad on, Snarley," he sez to me one day, "are nowt but matter and force." "Matter and force," I sez; "what's them?" And then he lets on for half a' hour trying to tell me all about matter and force. When he'd done I sez, "Tom Hankin, there's more sense in one o' them old shoes than there is in your silly 'ead. You've got things all wrong end up, and you're just baain' at 'em like a' old sheep!" "How can you prove it?" he sez. "I know it," I sez, "by the row you makes." it's a sure sign, sir; you take my word for it.

'Then there's all these parsons preaching away Sunday after Sunday. Why, doesn't it stand to sense that if they'd got things right way up, there they'd be, and that 'ud be the end on it? And it's because they're all wrong that they've got to go on jawin' to persuade people they're right. One day I was in Parson Abel's study. "What's all them books about?" I sez. "Religion, most on 'em," sez he. "Well," I sez, "if the folks as wrote 'em had got things right way up they wouldn't 'a needed to 'a wrote so many books."

'Then, agen, there's that professor as comes fishin' in summer. "Mr Dellanow," he sez to me one day, "I take a great interest in yer." "That's a darned sight more'n I take in you," I sez, for if there's one thing as puts my bristles up it's bein' told as folks takes a' interest in me. "Well," he sez, for he wasn't easy to offend, "I want to 'ave a talk." "What about?" I sez. "I want to talk about the stars and the space as they're floatin' in." "Has space ever knocked yer silly?" I sez. "Yes," he sez, "in a manner o' speakin' it has." "No," I sez, "it hasn't, because if it had you wouldn't want to talk about it." Well, there was no stoppin' 'im, and at last he gets it out that space is just a way we have o' lookin' at things. I know'd well enough what he meant, though I could see as he were puttin' it wrong way up. When he'd done

I sez, "That's all right. But suppose space wasn't a way folks have o' lookin' at things, but something else, what difference would that make?" "I don't see what you mean," he sez. "That's because you don't see what you mean yerself," I sez. "You're just like the rest on 'em—talkin' about things you've never seen, but only heard other folks talkin' about. You're in the same box wi' Shoemaker Hankin and the parsons and all the lot on 'em. What's the good o' jawin' about space when you've never been there yourself? I have. I've seen more space in one minute than you've ever heard talk on since you were born. Don't tell me! If you could see what I've seen you'd never say another word about space as long as yer lived."

'But you was askin' what bein' a medium has got to do wi' knowin' about the stars. More than some folks thinks. They're two roads leadin' to the same place. Both on 'em are ways o' gettin' to the right end of things. What's wrong wi' the mediums is that they haven't got *line* enough. They only manage to get just outside their own skins; but what's wanted is to get right on to the edge of the world and then look back. That's what the stars teaches you to do; and when you've done it—my word! it turns yer clean inside out!

'There's lots of nonsense in mediums; but there's no nonsense in the stars. And it's the stars that's goin' to knock the nonsense out o' the mediums, you mark my word! I found that out, for, as I was tellin' you, I used to be one myself, and am one now, for the matter o' that.

'Now you listen to what I'm goin' to tell you. There's lots o' spirits about: but they don't talk, at least not as a rule, and they don't want to talk; and when the mediums make 'em talk, they're liars! Spirits has better ways o' doin' things than talkin' on 'em. That's what you finds out when you gives yourself a long line and gets out to the edge o' the world. Then you looks back, and you sees that the whole thing's alive. It looks you straight in the face; and you can see it thinkin' and smilin' and frownin' and doin' things, just as I can see you at this minute. Do you think the stars can't understand one another? They can do it a sight better than you and me can. And they do it without speakin' a word. That, I tell you, is what you *sees* when you lets your line out to the edge!

'And when you've seen it you don't bother any more wi' makin' the spirits rap on tables and such like. What's the sense o' tryin' to find out whether you'll be a spirit after you're dead when you know there's nothing else anywhere? But it's no good talkin'. If you're not a bit of a medium yourself you'll never understand—no, not if I was to go on talkin' till both on us are frozen to death. And I reckon you're pretty cold already—you look it. Come down the hill wi' me, and I'll get my missis to make yer a cup o' hot tea.'

'SNARLEYCHOLOGY'

I. THEORETICAL

FARMER PERRYMAN was rich, and it was Snarley Bob who had made him so. Now Snarley was a cunning breeder of sheep. For three-and-forty years he had applied his intuitions and his patience to the task of producing rams and ewes such as the world had never seen. His system of 'observation and experiment' was peculiarly his own; it is written down in no book, but stands recorded on barn-doors, on gate-posts, on hurdles, and on the walls of a wheeled box which was Snarley's main residence during the spring months of the year. It is a literature of notches and lines—cross, parallel, perpendicular, and horizontal—of which the chief merit in Snarley's eyes was that nobody could understand it save himself. But it was enough to give his faculties all the aid they required. By such simple means he succeeded long ago in laying the practical basis of a life's work, evolving a highly complicated system controlled by a single principle, and yet capable of manifold application. The Perryman flock, now famous among sheep-breeders all over the world, was the result.

Thirty years ago this flock was the admiration and the envy of the whole countryside. Young farmers with capital were confident that they were going to make money as soon as they began to breed from the Perryman strain. To have purchased a Perryman ram was to have invested your money in a gilt-edged, but rising, stock. The early 'eighties' were times of severe depression in those parts; capital was scarce, farmers were discouraged, and the flocks deteriorated. At the present moment there is no more prosperous corner in agricultural England, and the basis of that prosperity is the life-work of Snarley Bob.

The fame of that work is now world-wide, though the author of it is unknown. The Perryman rams have been exported into almost every sheep-raising country on the globe. Hundreds of thousands of their descendants are now nibbling food, and converting it into fine mutton and long-stapled wool, in Canada, Australia, New Zealand, and the Argentine. Only last summer I saw a large animal meditating procreation among the foothills of the Rockies, and was informed of the fabulous price of his purchase—fabulous but commercially sound, for the animal was a Perryman ram, and the owner was sublimely confident of being 'up against a sure thing'. Many fortunes have been made from that source; and there are perhaps millions of human beings now eating mutton or wearing cloth who, if they could trace the authorship of these good things, would stand up and bless the memory of Snarley Bob.

One day among the hills I met the old man in presence of his charge, like a general reviewing his troops. As the flock passed on before us the professional reticence of Snarley was broken, and he began to talk of the animals before him, pointing to this and to that. Little by little his remarks began to remind me of something I had read in a book. On returning home, I looked the matter up. The book was a treatise on Mendelism, and, as I read on, the link was strengthened. Meeting Snarley Bob a few days afterwards, I did my best to communicate what I had learnt about Mendelism. He listened with profound attention, though, as I thought, with a trace of annoyance. He made some deprecatory remarks, quite in character, about 'learned chaps as goes 'umbuggin' about things they don't understand'. But in the end he was forced to confess some interest in what he had heard. 'Them fellers,' he said, 'is on the right road; but they don't know where they're goin', and they don't go far enough.' 'How much further ought they to go?' I asked. For answer Snarley pointed to rows of notches on a five-barred gate and said, 'It's all there.' Whether it is 'all there' or not I cannot tell; for the secret of these notches was never revealed to me, and the brain which held it lies under eight feet of clay in Deadborough churchyard. Perhaps Snarley is now discussing the matter with 'the tall Shepherd'[1] in some nook of Elysium where the winds are less than they used to be on Quarry Hill.

Had Snarley received a due share of the unearned increment

[1] See *post*, 'The Death of Snarley Bob'.

which his own and his rams' achievements brought into other hands he would probably have died a millionaire. But for all his toil and skill he received no more than a shepherd's wage. There were not wanting persons, of course, who regarded his condition as a crucial instance of the exceeding rottenness of our present industrial system. There was a great lady from London, named Lady Lottie Passingham, who resolved to take up the case. Lady Lottie belonged to the class who look upon the universe as a leaky old kettle and themselves as tinkers appointed by Providence to mend the holes. That Snarley's position represented a hole of the first magnitude was plain enough to Lady Lottie the moment she became acquainted with the facts. Her first step was to interest her brother, the Earl of Clodd, a noted breeder of pedigree stock, on the old man's behalf; her second, to rouse the slumbering soul of the victim to a sense of the injustice of his lot. I believe she succeeded better with her brother than with Snarley; for with him she utterly failed. Her discourse on the possibilities of bettering his position might as well have been spoken into the ears of the senior ram; and if the ram had responded, as he probably would, by pinning Lady Lottie against the wall of the barn, her overthrow would have been no more complete nor unmerited than that she actually received from Snarley Bob.

For it so happened that Providence, in equipping the lady for her world-mending mission, had forgotten to give her a pleasant voice. Now if there was one thing in the world which made Snarley 'madder' than anything else could do, it was the high-pitched, strident tones of a woman engaged in argument. The consequence was that his self-restraint broke down, and before the lady had said half the things she had meant to say, or come within sight of the splendid offer she was going to make on behalf of the Earl of Clodd, Snarley had spoken words and performed actions which caused his benefactress to retreat from the farmyard with her nose in the air, declaring she 'would have nothing more to do with the horrid brute'. She was not the first of Snarley's would-be benefactors who had formed the same resolve.

Now this extraordinary conduct on Snarley's part was by no means due to any transcendental contempt for money. I have myself offered him many a half-crown, which has never been refused; and Mrs Abel, unless I am much mistaken, has given him many a pound. Still less did it originate from rustic contentment with a humble lot; nor from a desire to act up to his catechism, by being satisfied with that station in life which Providence had assigned him. For there was no more restless soul within the four seas of Britain, and none less willing to govern his conduct by moral saws. And stupidity, which would probably have explained the facts in the case of any other dweller in those parts, was not to be thought of in Snarley's case. 'I knew what the old gal was drivin' at before she'd finished the text,' said Snarley to me.

The truth is that he was afflicted with an immense and incurable arrogance which caused him to resent the implication, by whomsoever offered, that he was worse off than other people. It was Snarley's distinction that he was able to maintain, and carry off, as much pride on eighteen shillings a week as would require in most people at least fifty thousand a year for effective sustenance. Of course, it was not the eighteen shillings a week that made him proud; it was the consciousness that he had inner resources which his would-be benefactors knew not of. He regarded them all as his inferiors, and, had he known how to do it, he would have treated them *de haut en bas*. Ill-bred insolence was therefore his only weapon; but his use of this was as effective as if it had been the well-bred variety in the hands of the grandest of grand seigneurs. No wonder, then, that he failed to achieve the position to which, in the view of Lady Lottie Passingham, his talents entitled him.

But the inner resources of which I have spoken were Snarley's sufficient compensation for his want of worldly success. The composition of this hidden bread, it is true, was somewhat singular and not easy to imitate. If the reader, when he has learned its ingredients, choose to call it 'religion', there is certainly nothing to prevent him. But that was not the word that Snarley used, nor the one he would have approved of. In his

own limited nomenclature the elements of his spiritual king-
dom were two in number—'the stars' and 'the spirits'.

Snarley's knowledge of the heavens was extensive, if not profound. On any fair view of profundity, I am inclined to think
that it was profound, though of the technique of astronomy he
knew but little. He had all the constellations at his fingers'
ends, and had given to many of them names of his own; he
knew their seasons, their days, even their hours; he knew the
comings and goings of every visible planet; by day and by
night the heavens were his clock. It was characteristic of him
that he seldom spoke of the weather when 'passing the time of
day'—a thing which he never did except to his chosen friends.
He spoke almost invariably of the planets or the stars. 'Good
morning, the sun's very low at this time o' year—did you see the
lunar halo last night?—a fine lot o' shootin' stars towards four
o'clock, look for 'em again to-morrow in the nor'-west—you can
get your breakfast by moonlight this week—Old Tabby [Orion]
looks well to-night—you'd better have a look at Sirius afore the
moon rises, I never see him so clear as he is now'—these were
the greetings which Snarley offered 'to them as could understand' from behind the hedge or within the penfold.

But it was not from superficialities of this kind that the depth
of his stellar interests was to be measured. I once told him that
a great man of old had declared that the stars were gods. 'So
they are, but I wonder how he found that out,' said Snarley;
'because you can't find it out by lookin' at 'em. You may look at
'em till you're blind, and you'll never see anything but little
lights.' 'It was just his fancy,' I said, like a simpleton. 'Fancy be
——!' said Snarley. 'It's a plain truth—that is, it's plain enough
for them as knows the way.'

'What's that?' I said.

'It's a way as nobody can take unless they're born to it. And,
what's more, it's a way as nobody can *understand* unless they're
born to it. Didn't I tell you the other day that there's only one
sort of folks as can tell what the stars are—and that's the folks
as can get out o' their own skins? And they're not many as can
do that. But that man you were just talkin' of, as said the stars

were gods, *he* must ha' done it. It's my opinion that in the old
days there was more folks as could get out o' their skins than
there are now. I sometimes wish *I'd* been born in the old days. I
should ha' had somebody to talk to then. I've got hardly anybody now. And you get tired sometimes o' keepin' yerself to
yerself. If I were a learned man I'd be readin' them old books
day and night.'

'What about the Bible?' I asked.

'Well, that's a good old book,' said Snarley; 'but there's
some things in it that's no good to anybody—*except to talkin'
men.*'

'Who are they?' I said.

'Why, folks as doesn't understand things, but only likes to
talk about 'em: parsons—at least, more nor half on 'em—ay, and
these 'ere politicians too, for the matter o' that. There's some
folks as dresses up in fine clothes, and there's some as dresses up
in fine words: one sort wants to be looked at, and the other
wants to be listened to. Doesn't it stand to sense that it's just the
same? Bless your 'eart, it's all *show*! Why, there's lots o' men as
goes huntin' about till they finds a bit o' summat as they think
'ud look well if they dressed it up in talk. "Ah," they says to
themselves, "that'll just do for me; that's what I'm goin' to *believe*; when it's got its Sunday clothes on it'll look like a regular
lord." Well, there's plenty o' that sort about; and you can allus
tell 'em by the 'oller sound as they makes. And them's the folks
as spoils the old Bible.

'Not but what there's things in the Bible as is 'oller to begin
wi'. But there's plenty that isn't, if these talkin' chaps 'ud only
leave it alone. Now, here's a bit as I calls tip-top: "When I con-
sider thy heavens, the work of thy fingers"' (here Snarley
quoted several verses of the Eighth Psalm).

'Now, when you gets hold on a bit like that, you don't want to
go dressin' on it up. You just puts it in your pipe and smokes it,
and then it does you good! *That's* it!

'There was once a Salvation Army man as come and asked
me if I accepted the Gospel. "Yes, my lad," I sez; "I've accepted
it—but only as a thing to *smoke*, not as a thing to go *bangin'*

about. Put your drum in the cupboard, my lad," I sez; "and put the Gospel in your pipe, and you'll be a wiser man."

'As for all this 'ere argle-bargling about them big things, *there's nowt in it,* you take my word for that! The little things for argle-bargle, the big 'uns for smokin', that's what *I* sez! Put the big 'uns in your pipe, sir; put 'em in your pipe, and smoke 'em!'

These last words were spoken in tones of great solemnity and repeated several times.

'That's good advice, Snarley,' I said; 'but the writer you just quoted hadn't got a pipe to put 'em in.'

'Didn't need one,' said Snarley; 'there weren't so many talkin' men about in his time. Folks then were born right end up to begin wi', and didn't need to smoke 'emselves round.

'Ay, ay, sir, I often think about them old days—and it's the Bible as set me thinkin' on 'em. That's the only old book as I ever read. And there's some staggerers in it, I can tell you! Wonderful! If some o' them old Bible men could come back and hear the parsons talkin' about 'em—eh, my word, there would be a rumpus! I'd like to see it, that I would! I'll tell you one thing, sir—and don't you forget it—you'll never understand the old Bible, leastways not the best bits in it, so long as you only wants to talk about 'em, same as a man *allus* wants to do when he's stuck inside his own skin. Now, there's that bit about the heavens, as I just give you—that's a bit o' real all-right, isn't it?'

'Yes,' I said, 'it is.'

'Well, can't you see as the man as said them words had just let himself out to the other end o' the line and was lookin' back? He'd got himself right into the middle o' the bigness o' things, and that's what you can't do as long as you keeps inside of your own skin. But I tell you that when you gets outside for the first time it gives you a pretty shakin' up. You begins to think what a fool you've been all your life long.'

Beyond such statements as these, repeated many times and in many forms, I could get no light on Snarley's dealings with the heavens.

To interpret his dealings with 'the spirits' is a still harder task. It was one of his common sayings that this matter also could not be discussed in terms intelligible to the once-born. That he did not mean by 'spirits' what the vulgar might suppose, is certain. It is true that at one time he used to attend spiritualistic séances held in a large neighbouring village, and he was commonly regarded as a 'medium'. This latter term was adopted by Snarley in many conversations I had with him as a true description of himself. But here again it was obvious that he used the term only for want of a better. He never employed it without some sort of caveat, uttered or implied, to the effect that the word must be taken with qualifications—unstated qualifications, but still suggestive of important distinctions.

It is noteworthy in this connection that a bitter quarrel existed between Snarley and the spiritualists with whom he had once been associated. They had cast him forth from among them as a smoking brand; and Snarley on his part never lost a chance of denouncing them as liars and rogues. One of the most violent scenes ever witnessed in the tap-room of the Nag's Head had been perpetrated by Snarley on a certain occasion when Shoemaker Hankin was defending the thesis that all forms of religion might now be considered as done for, 'except spiritualism'. Even Hankin, who reverenced no thing in heaven or earth, had protested against the unprintable words with which Snarley greeted his logic; while the landlord (Tom Barter of happy memory), himself the lowest blackguard in the village, had suggested that he should 'draw it mild'.

This reminds me that Snarley regarded strong drink as a means, and a legitimate means, for obtaining access to hidden things; nor did he scruple at times to use it for that end. 'There's nowt like a drop o' drink *for openin' the door*,' he remarked. 'But only for them as is born to it. If you're not born to it, drink shuts the door on you tighter nor ever. There's not one man in ten that drink doesn't make a bigger fool of than he is already. Look at Shoemaker Hankin. Half a pint of cider'll set him hee-hawin' like the Rectory donkey. But there's some men as can't get a lift no other way. It's like that wi' me sometimes. There's weeks and weeks together when I'm fair stuck inside my own skin and can't get out on it nohow. That's when I know a drop'll do me good. I can a'most hear something go click in my head, and then I gets among 'em (the spirits) 'in no time. A pint's mostly enough to do it; but sometimes it takes a quart; and once or twice I've had to go on till somebody's had to help me home. But when once I begins I never stops till I see the door openin'—and then not a drop more!'

II. EXPERIMENTAL

ONE day I was discussing with Mrs Abel the oft-recurrent problem of Snarley's peculiar mental constitution, a subject to
which she had given the name 'Snarleychology'.[1] Her knowledge of the old man's ways was of longer date than mine, and
she understood him infinitely better than I. 'Suppose, now,' I
said, 'that Snarley had been able to express himself after the
manner of superlative people like you and me, what would have
come of it?' 'Art,' said Mrs Abel, 'and most probably poetry.
He's just a mass of intuitions!' 'What a pity they are inarticulate!' I answered, repeating the appropriate commonplace.
'But they are not inarticulate,' said Mrs Abel. 'Snarley has
found a medium of expression which gives him perfect satisfaction.' 'Then the poems ought to be in existence,' said I. 'So they
are,' was the answer; 'they exist in the shape of Farmer Perryman's big rams. The rams are the direct creations of genius
working upon appropriate material. None but a dreamer of
dreams could have brought them into being; every one of them
is an embodied ideal. Don't make the blunder of thinking that
Snarley's sheep-raising has nothing to do with his star-gazings
and spirit-rappings. It's all one. Shakespeare writes *Hamlet*, and
Snarley produces "Thunderbolt".[2] To call Snarley inarticulate
because he hasn't written a *Hamlet* is as absurd as it would be
to call Shakespeare inarticulate because he didn't produce a
"Thunderbolt". Both *Hamlet* and "Thunderbolt" were born in
the highest heaven of invention. Both are the fruit of intuitions

[1] I suggested to Mrs Abel that this word wouldn't do, and proposed
'Snarleyology' instead. She declined the improvement at once, remarking
that 'the soul of the word was in the *ch*.'
[2] The name of the greatest of the Perryman rams—a brute 'with more
decorations than a Field-marshal'.

concentrated on their object with incredible pertinacity.'

I was forced into silence for a time, bewildered by a statement which seemed to alternate between levelling the big things down to the little ones, and raising the little ones to the level of the big. When I had chewed this hard saying as well as I could, I bolted it for further digestion, and continued the conversation. 'Has Snarley,' I asked, 'ever been tried with poetry, in the ordinary sense of the term?'

'Yes,' said the lady, 'an experiment was once made on him by Miss ——' (naming a literary counterpart to Lady Lottie Passingham), 'who visited him in his cottage and insisted on reading him some poem of Whittier's. In ten minutes she was fleeing from the cottage in terror of her life, and no one has since repeated the experiment.'

'I think,' I said, 'that if you would consent to be the experimenter we might obtain better results.'

Now in one important respect Nature had dealt more bountifully with Mrs Abel than with Lady Lottie Passingham. Though Mrs Abel had no desire to reform the universe, and was conscious of no mission to that end, she possessed a voice which might have produced a revolution. It was a soft contralto, vibrant and rich, and tremulous with tones which the gods would have come from Olympus to hear. She never sang, but her speech was music, rich and rare. In early life, as I have said, she had been on the stage, and Art had completed the gifts of Nature. Here lay one of the secrets of her power over the soul of Snarley Bob. Her voice was hypnotic with all men, and Snarley yielded to it as to a spell.

Another point which has its bearing on this, and also on what has to follow, is that Snarley had a passionate love for the song of the nightingale. The birds haunted the district in great numbers, and the time of their singing was the time when Snarley 'let out his line' to its furthest limits. His love of the nightingale was coupled, strangely enough, with a hatred equally intense for the cuckoo. To the song of the cuckoo in early spring he was fairly tolerant; but in June, when, as everybody knows, 'she changeth her tune'. Snarley's rage broke forth into bitter persecution. He had invented a method of his own, which I shall not divulge, for snaring these birds; and whenever he caught them he promptly wrung their necks. For the same reason he would have been not unwilling to wring the necks of Lady Lottie Passingham and of the Literary Counterpart had they continued to pester him.

Here then were the conditions from which we drew the materials for our conspiracy. Mrs Abel, though at first reluctant, consented at last to play the active part in a new piece of experimental Snarleychology. It was determined that we would try our subject with poetry, and also that we would try him with 'something big'. For a long time we discussed what this 'something big' was to be. Choice nearly fell on 'A Grammarian's Funeral', but I am glad this was not adopted; for, though it represented very well our own views of Snarley Bob, I doubt if it would have appealed directly to the subject himself. At length one of us suggested Keats' 'Ode to a Nightingale', to which the other immediately replied, 'Why didn't we think of that before?' It was the very thing.

But how were we to proceed? We knew very well that a deliberately planned attempt to 'read something' to Snarley was sure to fail. He would suspect that we were 'interested in him' in the way he always resented, or that we wanted to improve his mind, which was also a thing he could not bear. Still, we might practise a little artful deception. We might meet him together by accident in the quarry, as we had done before; and Mrs Abel, after due preliminaries and a little leading-on about nightingales, might produce the volume from her pocket and read the poem. So it was arranged. But I think we parted that night with a feeling that we were going to do something ridiculous, and Mr Abel told me quite frankly that we were a pair of precious fools.

One lovely morning about the middle of April the desired meeting in the quarry was duly brought off. The lambing season was almost over, and Snarley was occupied in looking after a few belated ewes. We arrived, of course, separately; but there must have been something in our manner which put

Snarley on his guard. He looked at us in turn with glances which plainly told that he suspected a planned attack on the isolation of his soul. Presently he lapsed into his most disagreeable manner, and his horse-like face began to wear a singularly brutal expression. It was one of his bad days; for some time he had evidently been 'stuck in his skin', and probably intended to end his incarceration that very night by getting drunk. He was in fact, determined to drive us away, and, though the presence of Mrs Abel disarmed him of his worst insolence, he managed to become sufficiently unpleasant to make us both devoutly wish we were at the bottom of the hill. I shudder to think what would have happened in these circumstances to Lady Lottie Passingham or to the Literary Counterpart.

The thing, however, had cost too much trouble to be lightly abandoned, and we did not relish the prospect of being greeted by peals of laughter if we returned defeated to the Rectory. In desperation, therefore, Mrs Abel began to force the issue. 'I'm told the nightingale was heard in the Rectory grounds last night, Snarley.' 'Nightingales be blowed,' replied the Subject. 'I've no time to listen if there was a hundred singin'. I've been up with these blessed ewes three nights without a wink o' sleep, and we've lost two lambs as were got by "Thunderbolt." ' 'Well, some time, when you are not quite so busy, I want you to hear what a great man has written about the nightingale,' said Mrs Abel. She spoke in a rather forced voice, which suggested the persuasive tones of the village curate when addressing a church-full of naughty children at the afternoon service.

'*I* don't want to hear it,' said Snarley, whose suspicions were now raised to certitude, 'and, what's more, I *won't* hear it. What's the good? If anybody's been talkin' about nightingales, it's sure to be rubbish. Nightingales is things you can't talk about, but only listen to. No, thank you, my lady. When I wants nightingales, I'll go and hear 'em. I don't want to know what nobody has said about 'em. Besides, I've too much to think about with these 'ere ewes. There's one lyin' dead behind them stones as I've got to bury. She died last night'; and he

began to ply us with disgusting details about the premature
confinement of a sheep.

It was all over. Mrs Abel remounted her horse, and presently
rode down the hill. When she had gone fifty yards or so, she
took a little calf-bound volume of Keats from her pocket and
held it aloft. The signal was not difficult to read. 'Yes,' it said,
'we *are* a pair of precious fools.'

Five months elapsed, during which I neither saw nor much
desired to see Mrs Abel. The harvest was now gathered, and the
event was to be celebrated by a 'harvest home' in the Perrymans' big barn. They were kind enough to send me the usual
invitation, which I accepted 'with pleasure'—a phrase in which,
for once in my frequent use of it, I spoke the truth. The
prospect of going down to Deadborough served, of course, to
revive the painful memory of our humiliating defeat. Looked
at in the perspective of time, our enterprise stood out in all its
essential folly. But I have frequently found that the con-
templation of a past mistake has a strange tendency to cause its
repetition; and it was so in this case. For it suddenly occurred
to me that this 'harvest home' might give us an opportunity for
a flank attack on the soul of Snarley Bob, whereby we might
retrieve the disaster of our frontal operations on Quarry Hill. I
lost no time in divulging my plan in the proper quarter. Mrs
Abel replied exactly as Lambert did when Cromwell, 'walking
in the garden of Brocksmouth House', told him of that sudden
bright idea for rolling up the Scottish army at Dunbar—'She
had meant to say the same thing.' The plan was simple enough;
but had its execution rested with any other person than Mrs
Abel—with the Literary Counterpart, for example—it would
have miscarried as completely as its forerunner.

The company assembled in the Perrymans' barn consisted of
the labouring population of three large farms, men and
women, all dressed in their Sunday best. To these were added,
as privileged outsiders, his Reverence and Mrs Abel, the popular stationmaster of Deadborough, Tom Barter—who supplied
the victuals—and myself. Good meat, of course, was in

abundance, and good drink also—the understanding with regard to the latter being that, though you might go the length
of getting 'pretty lively', you must stop short of getting drunk.

The proceedings commenced in comparative silence, the
rustics communicating with one another only by such whispers
as might be perpetrated in church. But this did not last very
long. From the moment the first turn was given to the tap in the
cider-barrel, the attentive observer might have detected a rapid
crescendo of human voices, which rose into a roar long before
the end of the feast. When all had eaten their fill, songs were
called for, and 'Master' Perryman, of course, led off with 'The
Farmer's Boy'.

Others followed. I was struck by the fact that nearly all the
songs were of an extremely melancholy nature—the chief
objects celebrated by the Muse being withered flowers, little
coffins, the corpses of sweethearts, last farewells, and hopeless
partings on the lonely shore. Tears flow; ladies sigh; voices
choke; hearts break; children die; lovers prove untrue. It was
tragic, and I confess I could have wept myself—not at the songs,
for they were stupid enough,—but to think of the grey, lug-
ubrious life whose keynote was all too truly struck by this
morbid, melancholy stuff.

Tom Barter, who had been in the army, and was just con-
valescent from a bad turn of *delirium tremens,* sang a song
about a dying soldier, visited on his gory bed by a succession of
white-robed spirits, including his little sister, his aged mother,
and a young female with a babe, whom the dying hero appeared to have treated none too well.

The song was vigorously encored, and Tom at once
responded with a second—and I have no doubt, genu-
ine—barrack-room ballad. The hero of this ditty is a 'Lancer
bold'. He is duly wetted with tears before his departure for the
wars; but is cheered up at the last moment by the lady's as-
surance that she will meet him on his return in 'a carriage gay'.
Arrived at the front, he performs the usual prodigies: slashes
his way through the smoke, spikes the enemy's guns, and spears
'Afghanistan's chieftains' right and left. He then returns to

England, dreaming of wedding-bells, and we next see him on the deck of a troopship, scanning the expectant throng on the shore and asking himself, 'Where, oh where, is that carriage gay?' Of course, it isn't there, and the disconsolate Lancer at once repairs to the 'smiling' village whence the lady had intended to issue in the carriage. Here he is met by 'a jet-black hearse with nodding plumes', seeks information from the weeping bystanders, and has his worst suspicions confirmed. He compares the gloomy vehicle before him with the 'carriage gay' of his dreams, and, having sufficiently elaborated the contrast, resolves to end his blighted existence on the lady's grave. How he spends the next interval is not told; but towards midnight we find him in the churchyard with his 'trusty' weapon in his hand. This, in keeping with the unities, should have been a lance; but apparently the Lancer was armed on some mixed principle known to the War Office, and allowed to take his pick of weapons before going on leave; for presently a shot rings out, and one of England's stoutest champions is no more.

During the singing of this song I noticed a poorly clad girl, with a sweet, intelligent face, put a handkerchief to her mouth and stifle a sob. She quietly made her way towards the barn door, and presently slipped out into the night.

The thing had not escaped the notice of Snarley Bob, and I could see wrath in his eyes. Being near him, I asked what it meant. 'By God!' he said, 'it's a good job for Tom Barter as the rheumatiz has crippled my old hands. If I could only double my fist, I'd put a mark on his silly jaw as 'ud stop him singing that song for many a day to come. Not that there's any sense in it. But it's just because there's no sense in 'em that such songs oughtn't to be sung. See that young woman go out just now? Well, she's in a decline, and knows as she can't last very long. And she's got a young man in India—in the same battery as our Bill—as nice and straight a lad as ever you see.'

Another song was called 'Fallen Leaves', the singer being a son of Peter Shott, the local preacher—a young man of dissipated appearance, with a white face and an excellent tenor voice. This song, of course, was a disquisition on the evanescence of all things here below. Each verse began 'I saw', and ended with the refrain:

'Fallen leaves, fallen leaves!
With woe untold my bosom heaves,
Fallen leaves, fallen leaves!'

'I saw,' said the song, a mixed assortment of decaying glories—among them, a pair of lovers on a seat, a Christmas family party, a rosebush, a railway accident on Bank Holiday, a rake's deathbed, a battlefield, an oak tree in its pride, and the same oak in process of being converted by an undertaker into a coffin for the poet's only friend. All these and many more the poet 'saw' and buried in his fallen leaves, assuring the world that his bosom heaved with woe untold for every one of them.

Tom Barter, who was the leading emotionalist in the parish, was visibly affected, his bosom heaving in a manner which the poet himself could not have excelled; while his poor anaemic wife, who had hesitated about coming to the feast because her eye was still discoloured from the blow Tom had given her last week, feebly expressed the hope 'that it would do him good'.

So it went on. Whatever jocund rebecks may have sounded in the England of long ago, their strains found no echoes in the funeral ditties of the Perrymans' feast.

Snarley Bob, in whom the drink had kindled some hankering for eternal splendours, was well content with the singing of 'The Farmer's Boy', and joined in the chorus with the remnants of a once mighty voice. After that he became restless and increasingly snappish; his face darkened at 'Fallen Leaves', and he began to look positively dangerous when a young man who was a railway porter in town, now home for a holiday, made a ghastly attempt at merriment by singing a low-class music-hall catch. What he would have done or said I do not know, for at that moment the announcement was made which the reader has been expecting—that Mrs Abel would give a recitation.

'Now,' said Snarley to his neighbour, 'we shall have summat like.' His whole being sprang to attention. He rapidly knocked out the ashes of his pipe, refilled, and lit; and, folding his arms before him on the table, leant forward to listen. For my part, I took a convenient station where I could watch Snarley, as Hamlet watched the king in the play. He was far too intent on Mrs Abel to notice me.

The barn was dimly lighted, and the speaker, standing far back from the end of the table, was in deep shadow and almost invisible. Has the reader ever heard a voice which trembles with emotions gathered up from countless generations of human experience—a voice in which the memories of ages, the designs of Nature, the woes and triumphs of evolving worlds become articulate; a voice that speaks a language not of words, but of things, transmuting the eternal laws to tones, and pouring into the soul by their means a stream of solicitations to the secret springs of the buried life? Such voices there are: Wordsworth heard one of them in the song of 'The Solitary Reaper'. In such a voice, rolling forth from the shadows, and in exquisite articulation, there came to us these words:

> 'My heart aches, and a drowsy numbness steals my sense,
>   As though of hemlock I had drunk,
>   Or emptied some dull opiate to the drains,
>   One minute past, and Lethewards had sunk.'

The noisy crew were hushed: silence fell like a palpable thing, Snarley Bob shifted his position: he raised his arms from the table, grasped his chin with his right hand; with his left he took the pipe from his mouth, and pointed its stem at the speaker; his features relaxed, and then fixed into the immobility of the worshipping saint.

Observation was difficult; for I, too, was half hypnotized by the voice from the shadows; but what I remember I will tell.

The voice has now finished the second verse, and is entering the third, the note slightly raised, and with a tone like that of a wailing wind:

> 'That I might drink and leave the world unseen,
>   And, with thee, fade away into the forest dim.
>
> *
>
>   Fade far away, dissolve, and quite forget
>   What thou among the leaves hast never known.'

Snarley Bob rises erect in his place, still holding his chin with his right hand, and with the left pointing his pipe, as before, at the speaker. The rigid arm is trembling violently, and Snarley, with half-open mouth, is drawing his breath in gulps. Someone, his wife I think, tries to make him sit down. He detaches his right hand, and violently thrusts her away.

For some minutes he remains in this attitude. The verse:

'Thou wast not born for death, immortal bird,'

is now reached, and I can see that violent tremors are passing through Snarley's frame. His head has sunk towards his breast, and is shaking; his right arm has fallen to his side, the fingers hooked as though he would clench his fist. Thus he stands, his head jerking now and then into an upright position, and shaking more and more. He has ceased to point at the speaker; the pipe is on the table. Thus to the end.

Somebody claps; another feebly knocks his glass on the board; there is a general whisper of 'Hush!' Snarley Bob has sunk on to the bench; he folds his arms on the table, rests his head upon them as a tired man would do; a tremor shakes him once or twice; then he closes his eyes, and is still. He had apparently fallen asleep.

No one, save myself, has paid much attention to Snarley, who is at the end of the room furthest from Mrs Abel. But now his attitude is noticed, and somebody says, 'Hullo, Snarley's had a drop too much this time. Give him a shake-up, missis.'

The 'shake-up', however, is not needed. For Snarley, after a few minutes of apparent sleep, raises his head, looks round him, and again stands upright. A flood of incoherencies, spoken in a high-pitched, whining voice, pours from his lips. Now and then comes a clear sentence, mingled with fragments of the poem—these in a startling reproduction of Mrs Abel's tones—thus: 'The gentleman's callin' for drink. Why don't they bring him drink?—Here, young woman, bring him a pint o' ale, and put three-ha'porth of gin in it—the door's openin', and he's goin' through. He'll soon be there—

> ' "Fade far away, dissolve, and quite forget
>   What thou among the leaves hast never known."

All right—it's bloomin' well all right—don't give him any more.

> ' "Now more than ever seems it rich to die,
>   To cease upon the midnight with no pain."

—It's the Passing Bell.—What are they ringing it for?—He's not dead—he'll come back again when he's ready.—Stop 'em ringing that bell!

> ' "Forlorn! the very word is like a bell
>   To toll me back from thee to my sole self."

All right—he's comin' back.—Nightingales!—Who wants to hear about a lot o' bloomin' nightingales. *I* don't. *I'm* all right—get me a cup o' tea.—It's Tom Barter who's drunk, not me!

> ' "Where beauty cannot keep her lustrous eyes,
>   Or new love pine at them beyond to-morrow."

The mail goes o' Fridays—K Battery, Peshawur, Punjab—O my God, let Bill tell him!—Shut up, you blasted old fool, or I'll knock yer silly head off! *You'll* never get there!—What do *you* know about nightingales? I heard 'em singin' for hundreds and thousands of years before *you* were born:

> ' "Thou wast not born for death, immortal bird,
>   No hungry generations tread thee down;
> The voice I heard this passing night was heard
>   In ancient days, by Emperor and clown:
> Perhaps the self-same voice that found a path
>   Through the sad heart of Ruth, when, sick for home,
>   She stood in tears amid the alien corn,
>   The same that oftimes hath
> Charmed magic casements, opening on the foam
>   Of perilous seas, in faery lands forlorn." '

The whole of this verse was a reproduction of Mrs Abel's rendering, spoken in a voice not unlike hers, and with scarcely the falter of a syllable. It was followed by a few seconds of incoherent babble, at the end of which tremors again broke out over Snarley's body; he swayed to and fro, and his head fell forward on his chest. 'Catch hold of him, or he'll fall,' cried somebody. Then a medley of voices—'Give him a drop of brandy!' 'No, don't you see he's dead drunk a'ready?' 'Drunk! not 'im. Do you think he could imitate Mrs Abel like that if he was drunk?' 'Take them gels out o' the barn as quick as you can!' 'If she don't stop shriekin' when you get her 'ome, throw a bucket o' cold water over her. It's only 'isterics.' 'Well, I've seed a lot o' queer things in my time, and I've knowed Snarley do some rum tricks, but I never seed nowt like *that*.' 'Oh dear, sir, I never felt so upset in all my life. It isn't *right*! Somebody ought to ha' stopped 'im. I wonder Mr Abel didn't interfere.' 'That there poem o' Mrs Abel's was a'most too much for me. But to think o' *him* gettin' up like that! It must be Satan that's got into him.' 'It's a awful thing to 'ave a man like that livin' in the next cottage to your own. I'll be frightened out o' my wits when my master's not at 'ome.' 'They ought to *do* something to 'im— I've said so many a time.'

And then the voice of Snarley's wife as she chafed her husband's hands: 'No, sir, don't you believe 'em when they say he's drunk. He's only had two glasses of cider and half a glass o' beer. You can see the other half in his glass now. I counted 'em myself. And it takes quarts to make 'im tipsy. It's a sort of trance, sir, as he's had. I've knowed him like this two or three times before. He was *just* like it after he'd been to hear Sir Robert Ball on the stars, sir—worse, if anythin'. He's gettin' better now; but I'm afraid he'll be terrible upset.'

Snarley had opened his eyes, and was looking vacantly and sleepily round him. 'I'll go home,' was all he said. He got up and walked rather shakily, but without assistance, out of the barn.

A few minutes later Mrs Abel came up to me. 'We were fools five months ago,' she said; 'but what are we now?'

'Criminals, most likely,' I replied.

'And if you do it again, you'll be murderers,' said Mr Abel, in a tone of severity.

A MIRACLE

I

In early life Chandrapál had been engaged in the practice of the law, and had held a position of some honour under the Crown. But as the years wore on the ties which bound him to the world of sense were severed one by one, and he was now released. By the study of the Vedanta, by ascetic discipline, and by the daily practice of meditation undertaken at regular hours, he had attained the Great Peace; and those who knew the signs of such attainment reverenced him as a holy man. His influence was great, his fidelity was unquestioned, and his fame as a teacher and sage had been carried far beyond his native land.

Chandrapál was versed in the lore of the West. He had studied the history, the politics, the literature and philosophy of the great nations, and could quote their poets and their sages with copiousness and aptitude. He had written a commentary on *Faust*. He also read, and sometimes expounded, the New Testament; and he held the Christian Gospel in high esteem.

Among the philosophers of the West it was Spinoza to whom he gave the place of highest honour. Regarding the Great Peace as the ultimate object of human attainment, he held that Spinoza alone had found a clear path to the goal; since then European thought had been continually decadent.

Though far advanced in life, Chandrapál had never seen Western civilization face to face until the year when we are about to meet him. He travelled to America by way of Japan, and Vancouver was the first Western city in which he set his foot. There he looked around him with bewildered eyes, gaining no clear impression, save in the negative sense that the city contained nothing to remind him of Spinoza or of the Nazarene. It was not that he expected to find a visible embodiment of their teaching in everything he saw; Chandrapál was too wise for that. But he hoped that somewhere and in some form the Truth, which for him these teachers symbolized in common, would show itself as a living thing. It might be that he would see it on some human face; or he might feel it in the atmosphere; or he might hear it in the voice of a man. Chandrapál knew that he had much to see and to discover; but in all his travels it was for this that he kept incessant watch.

From Vancouver he passed south to San Francisco; thence, city by city, he threaded his way across the United States and found himself in New York. All that he had seen so far gathered itself into one vast picture of a world fast bound in the chains of error and groaning for deliverance from its misery. In New York the misery seemed to deepen and the groanings to redouble. But of this he said nothing. He let the universities fête him; he let the millionaires entertain him in their great houses; he delivered lectures on the wisdom of the East, and, though a kindly criticism would now and then escape him, he gave no hint of his great pity for Western men. He was the most courteous, the most delightful of guests.

Arrived in England, he received the same impression and practised the same reserve. Wherever he went a rumour spread before him, and men waited for his coming as though the ancient mysteries were about to be unsealed. The curious cross-examined him; the bewildered appealed to him; the poor heard him gladly, and famished souls, eager for a morsel of comfort from the groaning table of the East, hovered about his steps. He preached in churches where the wandering prophet is welcomed; he broke bread with the kings of knowledge and of song; he sat in the seats of the mighty and received honour as one to whom honour is due.

To all this he responded with a gratitude which was sincere; but his deeper gratitude was for the Powers by whose ordering he had been born neither an Englishman nor a Christian, but a Hindu.

Here, as in America, he looked about him observingly, and pondered the meaning of what he saw. But he understood it

not, and went hither and thither like a man in a dream. In his
Indian home he had studied Western civilization from the
books which tell of its mighty works and its religion; and, so
studied, it had seemed to him an intelligible thing. But, seen
with the naked eye, it appeared incomprehensible, nay, incredible. Its bigness oppressed him, its variety confused him, its
restlessness made him numb. Values seemed to be inverted,
perspectives to be distorted, good and evil to be transposed: 'in'
meant 'out', and Death did duty for Life. Chandrapál could
not take the point of view, and finally concluded there was no
point of view to take. He could not frame his visions into co-
herence, and therefore judged that he was looking at chaos.
Sometimes he would doubt the reality of what he saw, and
would recollect himself and seek for evidence that he was
awake. 'Can such things be?' he would say to himself; 'for this
people has turned all things upside down. Their happiness is
misery, their wisdom is bewilderment, their truth is self-
deception, their speech is a disguise, their science is the parent
of error, their life is a process of suicide, their god is the worm
that dieth not and the fire that is not quenched. What is believed is not professed, and what is professed is not believed. In
yonder place'—he was looking at London—'there is darkness
and misery enough for seven hells. Verily they have already
come to judgment and been condemned.'

So thought Chandrapál. But his mistake, if it was one,
offended nobody; for he held his peace about these things.

There came a day when the folk of Deadborough were
startled from their wonted apathy by the apparition of a
Strange Man. They saw him first as he drove from the station
in a splendid carriage-and-pair, with a coronet on its panels.
Seated in the carriage was a venerable being with a swarthy
countenance and headgear of the whitest—such was the brief
vision. Other carriages followed in due course, for there was an
illustrious house-party at Deadborough Hall—the owner of
which was not only a slayer of pheasants, but a reader of books
and a student of things. He had gathered together the Bishop

of the Diocese, a Cabinet Minister, two eminent philosophers, the American Ambassador, a leading historian, and a Writer on the Mystics. To these was added—for he deserves a sentence to himself—an Orientalist of world-wide reputation. All were gathered for the purpose of meeting Chandrapál.

By the charm of his manners, by his urbanity, by his brilliant and thought-provoking conversation, the Oriental repaid his host a hundred times over. To most of his fellow-guests he played the part of teacher, while seeming to act that of disciple; but to none was his manner so deferential and his air of attention so profound as to the great Orientalist. And yet in the secret heart of Chandrapál this was the man for whom he felt the deepest compassion. He found, indeed, that the great man's reputation had not belied him; he was versed in the wisdom of the East and in the tongues which had spoken it; he knew the path to the Great Peace as well as the sage knew it himself; but when Chandrapál looked into his restless eyes and heard the hard tones of his voice, he perceived that no soul on earth was further from the Great Peace than this.

With the two philosophers Chandrapál spent many hours in close debate. He spoke to them of the Bhagavad Gita and of Spinoza. He found that of the Bhagavad Gita they knew little—and they cared less. Of Spinoza they knew much and understood nothing—thus thought he. So he turned to other topics and conversed fluently on the matters dearest to their hearts—namely, their own works, with which he was well acquainted. They, on their part, had never met a listener more sympathetic, a critic more acute. Chandrapál left upon them the impression of his immense capacity for assimilating the products of Western thought; also the belief that they had thoroughly rifled his brains.

Meanwhile he was thinking thus within himself: 'These men are keepers of shops, like the rest of their nation. Their merchandise is the thoughts of God, which they defile with wordy traffic, understanding them not. They have no reverence for their masters; their souls are poisoned with self; therefore the Light is not in them, and they know not the good from the evil.

The word of the Truth is on their lips, but it lives not in their hearts. Moreover, they are robbers; and even as their fathers stole my country so they would capture the secrets of my soul—that they may sell them for money and increase their traffic. But to none such shall the treasure be given. I will walk with them in the outer courts; but the innermost chamber they shall not so much as see.'

With the Cabinet Minister Chandrapál had this in common—that both were lawyers and servants of the Crown. Thus a basis of intercourse was established—were it only in the fact that each man understood the official reserve of the other. The first day of their acquaintance was passed by each in reconnoitring the other's position and deciding on a plan of campaign. The Minister concluded that there were three burning topics which it would be unwise to discuss with Chandrapál. Chandrapál perceived what these topics were, knew the Minister's reasons for avoiding them, and reflected with some satisfaction that they were matters on which he also had no desire to talk. His real object was to penetrate the Minister's mind in quite another direction, and he saw that this astute diplomatist had not the slightest suspicion of what he was after. This, of course, gave the tactical advantage to the Indian.

Now Chandrapál was more subtle than all the guests in Deadborough Hall. With great adroitness he managed to introduce the very topics on which, as he well knew, the Minister had resolved not to express himself; but he took care on each occasion to provide the other with an opportunity for talking about something else. This something else had been carefully chosen by Chandrapál, and it was a line of escape which led by very gradual approaches to the thing he wanted to find out. The Minister had won a great reputation in beating the diplomatists of Europe at their own game; but he had never before directly encountered the subtlety of an Oriental mind. Stepping aside from the dangerous spots to which the other was continually leading him, he put his foot on each occasion into the real trap; and thus, by the end of the third day, he had revealed what the Indian valued more than all the secrets of the British Cabinet. Meanwhile the Minister had conceived an intense dislike to Chandrapál, which he disguised under a mask he had long used for such purposes; at the same time he flattered himself on the ease with which he outwitted this wily man.

Chandrapál, on his side, reflected thus: 'Behold the misery of them that know not the Truth. This man flatters the people; but in his heart he despises them. Those whom he leads he knows to be blind, and his trade is to persuade them that they can see. The Illusion has made them mad; none sees whither he is going; the next step may plunge them all into the pit; they live for they know not what. All this is known to yonder man; and, being unenlightened, he has no way of escape, but yields to his destiny, which is, that he shall be the bond-servant of lies.' In short, the discovery which the Oriental believed himself to have made was this—that neither the Great Man before him, nor the millions whom he led, had the faintest conception of the Meaning of Life; and, further, that the Great Man was aware of his ignorance and troubled by it, whereas the millions knew it not and were at their ease.

With the Writer on Mystics he was reserved to the point of coldness. In this man's presence Chandrapál felt that he was being regarded as an 'interesting case' for analysis. So he wrapped himself in a mantle impervious to professional scrutiny, and gave answers which could not be worked up into a chapter for any book. The Writer was disappointed in Chandrapál, and Chandrapál had no satisfaction in the Writer. 'This man,' he thought, 'has studied the Light until he has become blind. He would speak of the things which belong to Silence. He is the most deeply entangled of them all.'

Fortunately for Chandrapál, there were children in the house, and these alone succeeded in finding the path to his heart. There was one Little Fellow of five years who continually haunted the drawing-room when he was there, hiding behind screens or the backs of armchairs, and staring at the Strange Man with wide eyes and finger in mouth. One day, when he was reading, the Little Fellow crept up to his chair on hands and knees and began industriously rubbing the dark wrist of the Indian with his wetted finger. 'It dothn't come off,' said the Little Fellow. From that moment he and the Strange Man became the fastest of friends and were seldom far apart.

Except for this companionship it may be said that never since leaving his native land was the spirit of Chandrapál more solitary nor more aloof from the things and the persons around him. Never did he despair so utterly of beholding that which he was most eager to find. Only when in the company of the Little Fellow, and in the hours reserved for meditation, was he able to shake off the sense of oppression and recover the balance of his soul. At these times he would quit the talkers and go forth alone into unfrequented places. Nowhere else, he thought, could a land be found more inviting than this to those moods of inward silence and content, whence the soul may pass, at a single step, into the ineffable beatitude of the Great Peace. Full, now, of the sense of harmony between himself and his visible environment, he would penetrate as far as he could into the forests and the hills. He would take his seat beside the brook; he would say to himself in his own tongue, 'This water has been flowing all night long,' and at the thought his mind would sink deep into itself; and presently the trees, the rocks, the fields, the skies, nay, his own body, would seem to melt into the movement of the flowing stream, and the Self of Chandrapál, freed from all entanglements and poised at the centre of Being, would gaze on the River of Eternal Flux.

One day, while thus engaged, standing on a bridge which carried a by-road over the stream, a shock passed through him: the stillness was broken as by thunder, the vision fled, and the entanglements fell over him like a gladiator's net. A motor, coming round a dangerous bend, had just missed him; and he stood covered with dust. Chandrapál saw and understood, and then, closing his eyes and making a mighty effort, shook the entanglements from his soul, and sank back swiftly upon the Centre of Poise.

The car stopped, and a white-haired woman alighted. A moment later there was a touch on the arm, and a human voice was calling to him from the world of shadows. 'I beg a thousand pardons,' said Mrs Abel; 'the driver was careless. Thank Heaven, you are unhurt; but the thing is an injury, and you are a stranger. My house is here; come with me, and you shall have water.'

What more was said I do not know. But when some hours later Chandrapál returned on foot to the Hall he walked lightly, for the load of pity had been lifted from his heart. To one who was with him he said: 'The Wisdom of the Nazarene still lives in this land, but it is hidden and obscure, and those who would find it must search far and long, as I have searched. Why are the Enlightened so few; for the Truth is simple and near at hand? The light is here, "but the darkness comprehendeth it not." Is not that so? The men in yonder house, who will soon be talking, are the slaves of their own tongues; but this woman with the voice of music is the mistress of her speech. They are of the darkness: she of the light. But perhaps,' he added, 'she is not of your race.'

Thus the Thing for which Chandrapál had never ceased to watch since his foot touched Western soil was first revealed to him; thus also the secret of his own heart, which he had guarded so long from the intrusion of the 'wise,' was first suffered to escape. He had lit his beacon and seen the answering fire.

Several months elapsed, during which Chandrapál continued his travels, visiting the capitals of Europe, interviewing German Professors, and seeing more and more of the Great Illusion (for so he deemed it) which is called 'Progress' in the West. He met reformers everywhere, and studied their schemes for amending the world; he heard debates in many parliaments, and did obeisance to several kings; he visited the institutions where day by day the wounded are brought from the battle, and where medicaments are poured into the running sores of Society; he went to churches, and heard every conceivable variety of Christian doctrine; he sat in the lecture-halls of socialists, secularists, anarchists, and irreconcilables of every sort; he made acquaintance with the inventors of new religions; he saw the Modern Drama in London, Paris, Berlin, and Vienna; he attended political meetings and listened to great orators; he was taken to reviews and beheld the marching of Armies and the manoeuvring of Fleets; he was shown an infinity of devices for making wheels go round, and was told of coming inventions that would turn them faster still. All these and many more such things passed in vision before him; but nothing stirred his admiration, nothing provoked his envy, nothing disturbed his fixed belief that Western civilization was an air-born bubble and a consummation not to be desired.

'The disease of this people is incurable,' he thought, 'because they are ignorant of the Origin of Sorrow. Hence they heal their woe at one end and augment its sources at the other. But as for me, I will hold my peace; for there is none here, no, not even the wisest, who would hear or understand. Never will the Light break forth upon them till the East has again conquered the West.'

A MIRACLE

WHEN all these things had been accomplished Chandrapál was again in Deadborough—a guest at the Rectory. It was Billy Rowe, an urchin of ten, who informed me of the arrival. Billy had just been let out of school, and was in the act of picking up a stone to throw at Lina Potts, whom he bitterly hated, when the Rectory carriage drove past the village green. At once every hand, including Billy's, went promptly to the corner of its owner's mouth, hoops were suspended in mid-career, and half-sucked lollipops, in process of transference from big sisters to little brothers, were allowed an interval for getting dry. The carriage passed; stones, hoops, and lollipops resumed their circulation, and by five o'clock in the afternoon the news of Chandrapál's arrival was waiting for the returning labourer in every cottage in Deadborough.

That night I repaired to the Nag's Head, for I knew that the arrival would have a favourable effect on the size of 'the house'. I am not addicted, let me say, to Tom Barter's vile liquors; but I have some fondness for the psychology of a village pub, and I was in hopes that the conversation in this instance would be instructive. An unusually large company was assembled, and to that extent I was not disappointed. But in respect of the conversation it must be confessed that I drew a blank. The tongues of the talkers seemed to be paralysed by the very event which I had hoped would set them all wagging. It was evident that every man present had come in the hopes that his neighbour would have something to say about Chandrapál, and thus provide an opening for his own eloquence. But nobody gave a lead, the whole company being apparently in presence of a speech-defying portent. At last I broke the ice by an allusion to the arrival. 'Ah,' said one, 'Oh,' said another. 'Indeed,' said a third.

'You don't say so,' said a fourth. At length one venturesome
spirit remarked, 'I hear as he's a great man in his own country.'
'I dare say he is,' replied the village butcher, with the air of one
to whom the question of human greatness was a matter of absolute indifference. That was the end. Shortly afterwards I left,
and presently overtook Snarley Bob, who had preceded me.
'Did you ever see such a lot o' tongue-tied lunatics?' said
Snarley. 'What made them silent?' I asked. 'They'd got too
much to say,' answered Snarley, and then added, rather mis-
chievously, 'They were only waitin' to begin till *you'd* gone. If
you was to go back now, you'd hear 'em barkin' like a pack o'
hounds.'

Among the many good offices for which Snarley had to
thank Mrs Abel, not the least was her systematic protection of
him from the intrusions of the curious. Plenty of people had
heard of him, and there were not wanting many who were
anxious to put his soul under the scalpel, in the interests of
Science. Mrs Abel was the channel through which they usually
attempted to act. But she knew very well that the thing was
futile, not to say dangerous. For some of the instincts of the
wild animal had survived in Snarley, of which perhaps the most
marked was his refusal to submit to the scrutiny of human
eyes. To study him was almost as difficult as to study the tiger
in the jungle. At the faintest sound of inquisitive footsteps he
would retreat, hiding himself in some place, or, more frequently, in some manner, whither it was almost impossible to
follow; and if, as sometimes happened, his pursuers pressed
hard and sought to drive him out of his fastness, he would
break out upon them in a way for which they were not prepared, and give them a shock which effectually forbade all
further attempts. Such a result was unprofitable to Science and
injurious to Snarley. For these reasons Mrs Abel had come to a
definite conclusion that the cause of Science was not to be advanced by introducing its votaries to Snarley Bob; and when
they came to the Rectory, as they sometimes did, she abstained
from mentioning his name, failed to answer when questioned,

and took care, so far as she could, that the old man should be left undisturbed.

But the reasons which led to this decision had no force in the case of Chandrapál. She was certain that Chandrapál would not treat Snarley as a mere abnormal specimen of human nature, a *corpus vile* for scientific investigation. She knew that the two men had something, nay, much, in common; and she believed that the ground of intercourse would be established the instant that Snarley heard the stranger's voice.

Nevertheless, the matter was difficult. It was well-nigh impossible to determine the conditions under which Snarley would be at his best, and, whatever arrangements were made, his animal shyness might spoil them all. To take him by surprise was known to be dangerous; and we had already found to our cost that the attempt to deceive him by the pretence of an accidental meeting was pretty certain to end in disaster. How Mrs Abel succeeded in bringing the thing off I don't know. There may have been bribery and corruption (for Snarley's character had not been formed from the fashion-books of any known order of mystics), and, though I saw nothing to suggest this method, I know nothing to exclude it—as a working hypothesis. But be that as it may, the arrangement was made that on a certain Wednesday evening Snarley was to come down to the Rectory and attend in the garden for the coming of Chandrapál. I had already learnt to regard Mrs Abel as a worker of miracles to whom few things were impossible; but this conquest of Snarley's reluctance to be interviewed, and in a manner so exceptional, has always impressed me as one of her greatest achievements. If the reader had known the old shepherd only in his untransfigured state—when, in his own phrase, he was 'stuck in his skin'—I venture to say he would as soon have thought of asking a grisly bear to afternoon tea in his drawing-room as of inviting Snarley Bob to meet an Indian sage in a rectory garden. But the arrangement was made—whether by the aid of Beelzebub or the attractions of British gold, no man will ever know.

Nothing in connection with Snarley had ever interested me

so much as the possible outcome of this strange interview; so that, when informed of what was going to happen, I sent a telegram to Mrs Abel asking permission to be on the spot—not, of course, as a witness of the interview but as a guest in the house. The reply was favourable, and on Tuesday afternoon I was at Deadborough.

I had some talk with Chandrapál, and I could see that he was not pleased at me coming. He asked me at once why I was there, and, on receiving a not very ingenuous answer, he became reserved and distant. Indeed, his whole manner reminded me forcibly of the bearing of Snarley Bob on the occasion of our ludicrous attempt on QuarryHill to introduce him to the poetry of Keats. I had come prepared to ask him a question; but I had no sooner reached the point than the whole fashion of the man was suddenly changed. His face, which usually wore an expression of quiet dignity, seemed to degenerate into a mass of coarse but powerful features, so that, had I seen him thus at a first meeting, I should have thought at once, 'This man is a sensualist and a ruffian!' His answers were distinctly rude; he said the question was foolish (probably it was)—that people had been pestering him with that kind of thing ever since he left India; in short, he gave me to understand that he regarded me as a nuisance. I had never before seen in him any approach to this manner; indeed, I had continually marvelled at his patience with fools, his urbanity with bores, and his willingness to give of his best to those who had nothing to give in return.

As the evening wore on he seemed to realize what he had done, and was evidently troubled. For my part, I had decided to leave next morning, for I thought that my presence in the house was disturbing him, and would perhaps spoil the chances of tomorrow's interview. Of this I had breathed no hint to anyone, and I was therefore greatly surprised when he said to me after dinner, 'I charge you to remain in this house. There is no reason for going away. I was not myself this afternoon; but it has passed and will not return. Come now, let us go out into the woods.'

Mrs Abel came with us. Her object in coming was to guide our walk in some direction where we were not likely to encounter Snarley Bob, whose haunts she knew, and whom it was not desirable that we should meet before the appointed time; for the nightingales were now in full song, and Snarley was certain to be abroad. We therefore took a path which led in an opposite direction to that in which his cottage lay.

Chandrapál had his own ways of feeling and responding to the influences of Nature—ways which are not ours. No words of admiration escaped him; but, on entering the woods where the birds were singing he said, 'The sounds are harmonious with thought.' There was no mistaking the hint.

Guided by the singing of the birds, we turned into an unfrequented lane, bordered by elms. The evening was dull, damp, and windless, and the air lay stagnant between the high banks of the lane. We walked on in complete silence, Chandrapál a few yards in front; none of us felt any desire to speak. Three nightingales were singing at intervals: one at some distance in the woods ahead of us, two immediately to our right. Whether it was due to the dampness in the air or the song of the birds, I cannot tell; but I felt the 'drowsy numbness', of which the poet speaks, stealing upon me irresistibly. We presently crossed a stile into the fields; and as I sat for a moment on the rail the drowsiness almost overcame me, and I wondered if I could escape from my companions and find some spot whereon to lie down and go to sleep. It required some effort to proceed, and I could see that Mrs Abel was affected in a similar manner.

By crossing the stile we had disturbed one of the birds, and we had to wait some minutes before its song again broke out much further to the right. For some reason of his own Chandrapál had found this bird the best songster of the three; and, wishing to get as near as possible, he again led the way and gave us a sign to follow. We cautiously skirted the hedge, making our way towards a point on the opposite side of the field where there was a gate, and beyond this, in the next field, a shed of some sort where we might stand concealed.

We passed the gate, turned into the shed, and were immediately confronted by Snarley Bob.

Both Mrs Abel and I were alarmed. We knew that Snarley Bob when disturbed at such a moment was apt to be exceedingly dangerous, and we remembered that it was precisely such a disturbance as this which had brought him some years ago within measurable distance of committing murder. Nor was his demeanour reassuring. The instant he saw us, he rose from the shaft of the cart on which he had been seated, smoking his pipe, and took a dozen rapid steps out of the shed. Then he paused, just as a startled horse would do, turned half round, and eyed us sidelong with as fierce and ugly a look as any human face could wear. Then he began to stride rapidly to and fro in front of the shed, stamping his feet whenever he turned, and keeping his eyes fixed on the swarthy countenance of Chandrapál, with an expression of the utmost ferocity.

Chandrapál retained his composure. Whatever sudden shock he may have felt had passed immediately, and he was now standing in an attitude of deep attention, following the movement of Snarley Bob and meeting his glance without once lowering his eyes. His calmness was infectious. I felt that he was master of the situation, and I knew that in a few moments Snarley's paroxysm would pass.

It did pass; but in a manner we did not expect. Snarley, on his side, had begun to abate his rapid march; once or twice he hesitated, paused, turned round; and the worst was already over when Chandrapál, lifting his thin hands above his head, pronounced in slow succession four words of some strange tongue. What they meant I cannot tell; it is not likely they formed any coherent sentence: they were more like words of command addressed by an officer to troops on parade, or by a rider to his horse. Their effect on Snarley was instantaneous. Turning full round, he drew himself erect and faced us in an attitude of much dignity. Every trace of his brutal expression slowly vanished; his huge features contracted to the human size; the rents of passion softened into lines of thought; wisdom and benignity sat upon his brows; and he was calm and still as the Sphinx in the desert.

Snarley stood with his hands linked behind his back, looking straight before him into the distance; and Chandrapál, without changing his attitude, was watching him as before. As the two men stood there in silence, my impression was, and still is, that they were in communication, through filaments that lie hidden, like electric cables, in the deeps of consciousness. Each man was organically one with the other; the division between them was no greater than between two cells in a single brain; the understanding was complete. Thus it remained for some seconds; then the silence was broken by speech, and it was as though a cloud had passed over the sun. For, with the first word spoken, misunderstanding began; and, for a time at all events, they drifted far apart, each out of sight and knowledge of the other's soul. Had Snarley begun by saying something inconsequent or irrelevant, had he proposed to build three tabernacles, or cried, 'Depart from me, for I am a sinful man,' or quoted the words of some inapplicable Scripture that was being fulfilled—there might have been no rupture. But, as it was, he spoke to the point, and instantly the tie was snapped.

'Them words you spoke just now,' he said, and paused. Then, completing the sentence—'them words was full o' *sense*.'

I could see that Chandrapál was troubled. The word 'sense' woke up trains of consciousness quite alien to the intention of the speaker. To his non-English mind this usage of the word, if now unknown, was at least misleading.

He replied, 'Those words have nothing to do with "sense." Yet you seemed to understand them.'

'Not a bit,' said Snarley. 'But I *felt* 'em. They burnt me like fire. Good words is allus like that. There's some words wi' meanin' in 'em, but no sense; and they're fool's words, most on 'em. You understand 'em, but you don't feel 'em. But when they comes wi' a bit of a smack, I knows they're all right. You can a'most taste 'em and smell 'em when they're the right sort—just like a drop o' drink. It's a pity you didn't hear Mrs Abel when she give us that piece o' poetry. That's the sort o' words folks ought to use. You can feel 'em in your bones. Well, as I was a sayin', your words was like that. They come at me smack, smack. And I sez to myself as soon as I hears 'em, "That's a man worth talkin' to." '

Chandrapál had listened with the utmost gravity, seeming to catch Snarley's drift. The diction must have puzzled him, but I doubt if the subtlest skill in exposition would have availed Snarley half so well in restoring the mutual comprehension which had been temporarily broken. Chandrapál was evidently relieved. For half a minute there was silence, during which he walked to and fro, deep in thought. Then he said, 'Great is the power of words when the speaker is wise. But the Truth cannot be *spoken.*'

'Not *all* on it,' said Snarley, 'only bits here and there. That's what the bigness o' things teaches you. It's my opinion as there are two sorts o' words—shutters-in and openers-out. Them words 'o yours was openers-out; but most as you hears are shutters-in. It's like puttin' a thing in a box. You shuts the lid, and then all you sees is the box. But when things get beyond a certain bigness you can't shut 'em in—not unless you first chops 'em up, and that spoils 'em.

'Now, there's Shoemaker Hankin—a man as could talk the hindleg off a 'oss. He goes at it like a hammer, and thinks as he's openin' things out; but all the time he's shuttin' on 'em in and nailin' on 'em up in their coffins. One day he begins talkin' about "Life", and sez as how he can explain it in half a shake. "You'll have to kill it first, Tom," I sez, "or it'll kick the bottom out o' *your* little box." "I'm going to *hannilize* it," he sez. "That means you're goin' to chop it up," I sez, "so that it's bound to be dead before we gets hold on it. All right, Tom, fire away! Tell us all about dead Life."

'Well, that's allus the way wi' these talkin' chaps. There was that Professor as comes tellin' me what space were—I told that gentleman' (pointing to me) 'all about *him.* Why, you might as well try to cut runnin' water wi' a knife. Talkin' people like him are never satisfied till they've trampled everything into a *muck*—same as the sheep tramples the ground when you puts 'em in a pen. They seems to think as that's what things are *for*! They all wants to do the talkin' themselves. But doesn't it stand to sense that as long as you're talkin' about things you can't hear what things are sayin' to you?

'When did I learn all that? Why, you don't *learn* them things. You just finds 'em, when you're alone among the hills and the bigness o' things comes over you. Do you know anything about the stars? Well, then, you'll understand.

'All the same, I were once a talkin' man myself; ay, and it were then as I got the first lesson in leavin' things alone. It happened one day when I were a Methody—long before I knew anything about the stars. I'd been what they call "converted"; and one day I were prayin' powerful at a meetin', and we was all excited, and shoutin' as we wouldn't go home till the answer had come. Well, it did come—at least it come to me. I were standin' up shoutin' wi' the rest, when all of a sudden I kind o' heard somebody whisperin' in my ear. "The answer's comin'," I sez; "I'm gettin' it." So they all gets quiet, waitin' for me to give the answer. I suppose they expected me to say as a new heart had been given to somebody we'd been prayin' for. But instead o' that I shouts out at the top o' my voice—though I can't tell what made me do it—"Shut up, all on you! Shut up, Henry Blain! Shut up, John Scarsbrick! Shut up, Robert Dellanow— *I'm tired o' the lot on you!*" That's what made me give up bein' a Methody. I began to see from that day that when things begins to open out you've got to *shut up*.'

'The voices of the world are many; and the speech of man is only one,' said Chandrapál.

'You're right,' said Snarley, 'but I'm not sure as you ought to call 'em voices. Most on 'em's more like faces nor voices. It's true there's the thunder and the wind—'specially when it's blowin' among the trees. And then there's the animals and the birds.'

'It is said in the East that once there were men who understood the language of birds.'

'No, no,' said Snarley, 'there's no understandin' them things. But there's one bird, and that's the nightingale, as makes me

kind o' remember as I understood 'em once. And there's no
doubt they understand one another; and there's some sorts of
animals as understands other sorts—but not all. You can take
my word for it!'

The light had failed, and the song of the birds, driven to a
distance by our voices, seemed to quicken the darkness into life.
"Darkling, we listened"—how long I know not, for the sub-
liminal world was awake, and the measure of time was lost.
Snarley was the first to speak, taking up his parable from the
very point where he had left it, as though he were unconscious
that a long interval had elapsed. He spoke to Chandrapál.

'I can see as you're a rememberin' sort o' gentleman,' he said.
'If you weren't, you wouldn't ha' come here listenin' to the
birds. The animals remember a lot o' things as we've forgotten.
I dare say you know it as well as I do. Now, there's the nightingale—*that's* the bird for recollectin' and makin' you recollect;
and you might say dogs and 'osses too. You can see the memory
in the dog's eyes and in the 'oss's face. But you can *hear* it in
the bird's voice—and hearin' and smellin' is better nor seein'
when it comes to a matter o' rememberin'.

'Yes, and it's my opinion as animals, takin' 'em all round, are
wiser nor men—that is, they've got more sense. You let your line
out far enough, and I tell you there's some animals as can make
you find a lot o' things as you've forgotten. That's what the bird
does. When I listens, I seems to be rememberin' all sorts o'
things, only I can't tell nobody what they are.

'Yes, but you ought to ha' been here that night when Mrs
Abel give that piece! Why, bless you, she'd got the nightingale
to a T, especially the rememberin'. Eh, my word, but it were a
staggerer! I *wish* you'd been there—a rememberin' gentleman
like you! You get her to give you that piece when you goes
home, and it'll make you reel your line out to the very end.'

Some of those allusions, I imagine, were lost on Chandrapál.
But once more he showed that he caught the 'sense'.

'In my country,' he said, 'religion forbids us to take the lives
of animals.'

'That's a good sort o' religion,' said Snarley. 'There's some sense in that! Them as holds with it must ha' let their line out pretty far. Now, it wouldn't surprise me to hear as folks in your country are good at rememberin' things as other folks have forgotten.'

'Yes, some of us think we can remember many things.' And, after a pause, 'I thought just now that I remembered you.'

'And me you!' said Snarley, 'blessed if I didn't. The minute you said them funny words, danged if I didn't feel as though I'd knowed you all my life! It was just like when I'm listenin' to the bird—all sorts o' things comes tumblin' back. Same with them words o' yours. It seemed as though somebody as I knowed were a-callin' of me. I must ha' travelled millions o' miles, same as when you lets your line out to the stars. And all the time I were sure that I knowed the voice, though I couldn't understand the meanin'. I tell you, it were *just* like listenin' to the bird.'

Chandrapál now turned and said something to Mrs Abel. She promptly slipped out of the shed, giving me a sign to follow. Chandrapál and Snarley were left to themselves.

*

Late at night Chandrapál returned to the Rectory. He was more than usually silent and absorbed. Of what had passed between him and Snarley he said not a word; but, on bidding us good-night, he remarked to Mrs Abel, 'The cycle of existence returns upon itself.' And Snarley, on his part, never spoke of the occurrence to any living soul. 'The rest is silence.'

SHEPHERD TOLLER O'
CLUN DOWNS

At the age of fifty or thereabouts Shepherd Toller went mad. After due process he was handed over to the authorities and graduated as a pauper lunatic. His madness was the outcome of solitude, and it was not surprising that, after a year amid the jovial company of the asylum, Toller began to improve. At the end of the second year he was declared to be cured, and discharged, much to his regret.

His first act on liberation was to recover his old dog, which had been left in charge of a friend. Desiring to start life again where his former insanity would be unknown, he made his way to Deadborough, the village of his birth. Arrived there, after a forty miles' walk, he refreshed himself with a glass of beer and a penn'orth of bread and cheese, and proceeded at once to Farmer Perryman in quest of work. The farmer, who was, as usual, in want of labour, sent him to Snarley Bob to 'put the measure on him'. Snarley's report was favourable. 'He seemed a bit queer, no doubt, and kept laughin' at nothin'; but I've knowed lots o' queer people as had more sense than them as wasn't queer, and there's no denyin' as he's knowledgeable in sheep.' The result was that Toller was forthwith appointed as an understudy to Snarley Bob.

Bob's estimate of the new-comer rose steadily day by day. 'He had a wonderful eye for points.' 'As good a sheep-doctor as ever lived.' 'Wanted a bit of watchin', it was true, but had a head on his shoulders for all that.' 'Knows how to keep his mouth shut.' 'Was backward in breedin', but not for want o' sense—hadn't caught him young enough.' 'Could ha' taught him anything, if he'd come twenty-five years back.' In due course, therefore, Toller was entrusted with great responsibilities. He it was who, under Snarley's direction, presided over the generation, birth, and early upbringing of the thrice-renowned 'Thunderbolt'.

So it went on for three years. At the end of that time Toller had an accident. He fell through the aperture of a feeding-loft, and his spinal column received an ugly shock. Symptoms of his old malady began to return. He began to get things 'terrible mixed up', and to play tricks which violated both the letter and the spirit of Snarley's notches.

One of the breeding points in Snarley's system was connected with the length of the lambs' ears. Short ears in the new-born lamb were prophetic of desirable points which would duly appear when the creature became a sheep; long ears, on the other hand, indicated that the cross had failed. A crucial experiment on these lines was being conducted by aid of a ram which had been specially imported from Spain, and the whole thing had been left to Toller's supervision. The result was a complete failure. On the critical day, when Snarley returned from his obstetric duties, his wife saw gloom and disappointment on his countenance. 'Well, have them lambs come right?' 'Lambs, did you say? They're not *lambs*. They're young *jackasses*. It's summat as Shepherd Toller's been up to. You'll never make me believe as the Spanish ram got any one on 'em—no, not if you was to take your dyin' oath. Blessed if I know where he found a father for 'em. It's not one o' our rams, I'll swear. You mark my word, missis, Shepherd Toller's goin' out of his mind again. I've seen it comin' on for months. Only last Tuesday he sez to me, "Snarley, I'm gettin' cloudy on the top." '

Shortly after this Toller disappeared and, though the search was diligent, he could not be found. 'He's not gone far,' said Snarley. 'Leastways he's sure to come back. Madmen allus comes back.' And within a few months an incident happened which enabled Snarley to verify his theory. It came about in this wise.

A party of great folk from the Hall had gone up into the hills for a picnic. They had chosen their camp near the head of a long upland valley, where the ground fell suddenly into a deep gorge pierced by a torrent. A fire of sticks had been lit close to the edge of the precipice, and a kettle, made of some shining metal, had been hung over the flames. The party were standing by, waiting for the water to boil, when suddenly, crash!—a sprinkle of scalding water in your face—and—where's the kettle? An invisible force, falling like a bolt from the blue, had smitten the kettle and hurled it into space. The ladies screamed; the Captain swore; the Clergyman cried, 'Good Gracious!' the Undergraduate said, 'Jerusalem!' the Wit added, '*And* Madagascar!' But what was said matters not, for the Recording Angel had dropped his pen. The whole party stood amazed, unable to place the occurrence in any sort of intelligible context, and with looks that seemed to say, 'The reign of Chaos has returned, and the Inexpressible become a fact!' Some went to the edge of the gorge and saw below a mass of buckled tin, irrecoverable, and worthless. Some looked about on the hillside, but looked on nothing to the point. Some stood by the spot where the kettle had hung, and argued without premisses. Some searched for the missile, some for the man; but neither was found. The whole thing was an absolute mystery. The party had lost their tea, and gained a subject for conversation at dinner. That was all.

That night Snarley, in the tap-room of the Nag's Head, heard the story from the groom who had lit the fire, hung the kettle, and seen it fly into space. Snarley said nothing, quickly finished his glass, and went home. 'Missis,' he said, 'get my breakfast at three o'clock to-morrow morning. Shepherd Toller's come back. And mind you hold your tongue.'

By five o'clock next morning Snarley had reached the scene of the picnic. He gazed about him in all directions: nothing was stirring but the peewits. Then he climbed down the gorge with some difficulty, found the kettle, and examined its riven side. Climbing back, he went some distance further up the valley, ascended a little knoll, took out his whistle, and blew a peculiar blast, tremulous and piercing. No response. Snarley blew again, and again. At the fourth attempt the distant barking of a dog was heard, and a minute later the signal was answered by the counterpart to Snarley's blast. Presently the form of a big man, followed by a yelping dog, appeared on the skyline above. Shepherd Toller was found.

During the week which followed these events, various members of the picnic-party had begun to recollect things they had previously forgotten, and discoveries were made, *ex post facto,* which warranted the submission of the case to the Society for the Investigation of Mysterious Phenomena. Lady Lottie Passingham had been of the party, and she it was who drew up the Report which was so much discussed a few years ago. In her own evidence Lady Lottie, whose figure was none too slim, averred that, as she climbed the hill to the place of rendezvous, she had been distinctly conscious of something pulling her back. She had attached no importance to this at the time, though she had remarked to Miss Gledhow that she wished she hadn't come. The time at which the kettle flew was 4.27 p.m.; at 4.25 Lady Lottie had a sensation as though a cold hand were stroking her left cheek, the separate fingers being clearly distinguishable. Miss Gledhow had experienced a feeling all afternoon that she was being *watched and criticized*—a feeling which she could only compare to that of a person who is having his photograph taken. Captain Sorley's cigarettes kept going out in the most unaccountable manner; and in this connection he would mention that more than once, and especially a few minutes after the main occurrence, he could not help fancying that someone was breathing in his face. The Rev. E. F. Stark-Potter had heard, several times, a sound like 'Woe, woe,' which he attributed at first to some ploughman calling to his horses; subsequent inquiry had proved, however, that, on the day in question, no ploughing was being done in the neighbourhood. All the witnesses concurred in the statement that they were vividly conscious of *something wrong,* the most emphatic in this respect being the Undergraduate, who had made no secret of his feeling at the time by assuring several members of the party that he felt absolutely 'rotten'. Further, the Report stated, the scene had been identified with the spot where a young woman committed suicide in 1834 by casting herself down the precipice. The battered kettle was also recovered and sent in a registered parcel for examination by the experts of the Society.

After the mature deliberation due to the distinguished names at the end of the Report, the Society decided that the evidence was non-veridical, and refused to print the document in their *Proceedings*.

Snarley Bob, who knew what was going on, had his reasons for welcoming this development. He concocted various legends of his own weird experiences at the valley-head, and these, as coming from him, had considerable weight. They were communicated in the first instance to the groom. By him they were conveyed to the coachman; by him, to the coachman's wife; whence they were not long in finding their way, by the usual channels, to headquarters. Here the contributions of Snarley were combined by various hands into an artistic whole with the original occurrence, which, in this new context, at once quitted the low ground of History and began a free development of its own in the realms of the Ideal. By the time it reached the Press it had become a fiction far more imposing than any fact, and far more worthy of belief. Things that never happened filled the foreground, and the thing that did happen had fallen so far into the background as to be almost invisible. The incident of the kettle had exfoliated into a whole sequence of imposing mysteries, becoming in the process a mere germ or point of departure of no more significance in itself than are the details in Saxo Grammaticus to a first-class performance of *Hamlet*. Thus transfigured, the story was indeed a drama rather than a narrative; and those who remember reading it in that form will hardly believe that it had its origin in the humble facts which these pages relate. The excitement it caused lasted for some weeks, and it was almost a public disappointment when the Society for the Investigation of Mysterious Phenomena blew a cold blast upon the whole thing.

When Snarley Bob met Shepherd Toller at Valley Head, he found him accoutred in a manner which verified his private theory as to the levitation of the kettle. Coiled round Toller's left arm were three slings, made from strips of raw oxhide, with pouches, large and small, for hurling stones of various size. Slung over his back was a big bag, also of leather, which contained his ammunition—smooth pebbles gathered from the torrent bed, the largest being the size of a man's fist. Strapped round his waist was a flint axe, the head being a beautiful celt, which Toller had discovered long ago on Clun Downs, and skilfully fixed in a handle bound with thongs.

In the days of Toller's first madness, it had been his habit to wander over Clun Downs, equipped in this manner. He had lived in some fastness of his own devising, and supplied his larder by the occasional slaughter of a stolen sheep, whose skull he would split with a blow from the flint-axe. The slings were rather for amusement than hunting, though his markmanship was excellent, and he was said to be able at any time to bring down a rabbit, or even a bird. All day long he would wander in unfrequented uplands, slinging stones at every object that tempted his eye, and roaring and dancing with delight whenever he hit the mark. He was inoffensive enough and had never been known to deliberately aim at a human being, though more than one shooting party had been considerably alarmed by the crash of Toller's stones among the branches, or by his long-range sniping of the white-clothed luncheon-table. On one occasion Toller had landed a huge pebble, the size of an eight-pounder shot, into the very bull's-eye of the feast—to wit, a basket containing six bottles of Heidsieck's Special Reserve. It was this performance which led Sir George to report the case to the authorities and insist on Toller being put under restraint.

By the evening of the day when Toller disappeared from the Perryman sheepfolds he had completed the long walk to his former haunts, and recovered his weapons from under the cairn where he had carefully hidden them six years before. The axe, of course, was uninjured; but the slings were rotten. As soon as it was dark, therefore, Toller stole down to the pastures, captured a steer, brained it with the flint axe, stripped off the skin, made a fire, roasted a piece of the warm flesh, covered his tracks, and before the sun was up had made twenty miles of the return journey, with half a dozen fine new slings concealed beneath his coat. He arrived at Deadborough at nightfall the day but one following, having taken a circuitous route far from the highroad. He at once made his way into the hills.

Beyond the furthest outposts of the Perryman farm lie extensive wolds rising rapidly into desolate regions where sheep can scarcely find pasture. In this region Toller concealed himself. About two miles beyond the old quarry, on a slaty hillside, he found a deep pit, which had probably been used as a water-hole in prehistoric times; and here he built himself a hut. He made the walls out of the stones of a ruined sheep-fold; he roofed them with a sheet of corrugated iron, stolen from the outbuildings of a neighbouring farm, and covered the iron with sods; he built a fireplace with a flue, but no chimney; he caused water from a spring to flow into a hollow beside the door. Then he collected slate, loose stones, and earth; and, by heaping these against the walls of the hut, he gave the whole structure the appearance of a mound of rubbish. Human eyes rarely came within sight of the spot; but even a keen observer of casual objects would not have suspected that the mound represented any sort of human dwelling. It was a masterpiece of protective imitation, an exact replica of Toller's previous abode on Clun Downs. His fire burned only by night.

The furnishing of this simple establishment consisted of a feather bed, which rested on slabs of slate supported by stones,—whence obtained was never known, but undoubtedly stolen. The coverlet was three sheepskins sewn together, the pillow also a sheepskin, coiled round a cylinder of elastic twigs. The table was a deal box, once the property of Messrs Tate, the famous refiners of sugar. The chair was a duplicate of the table. The implements were all of flint, neatly bound in their handles with strips of hide. There was the axe for slaughter, a dagger for cutting meat, a hammer for breaking bones, a saw and scrapers of various size—the plunder of some barrow on

Clun Downs. Under the slates of the bed lay a collection of slings.

In this place Toller lived undiscovered for several months, issuing thence as occasion required in quest of food. This he obtained by night forays upon distant farms, bringing back mutton or beef, lamb or sucking pig, a turkey, a goose, a couple of chickens, according to the changes of his appetite or the seasonableness of the dish. Fruit, vegetables, and potatoes were obtained in the same manner. In addition, all the game of the hills was at his mercy, and he had fish from the stream. It was characteristic of Toller's cunning that his plunder was all obtained from afar, and seldom twice from the same place. He would go ten miles to the north to steal a lamb; next time, as far to the south to steal a goose. The plundered area lay along the circumference of great circles, with radii of ten, fifteen, twenty miles, of which his abode was the centre. This put pursuers off the track, and caused them to look for him everywhere but where he was. The police were convinced, for example, that he was hiding in Clun Downs. The steer he had slaughtered on his first return had been discovered, as Toller intended it to be; and, in order to keep up the fiction of his presence in that neighbourhood, he repeated his exploit a month later, and slaughtered a second steer in the very pasture where he had killed the first.

Nor was his favourite amusement denied him. He knew the movements of every shepherd on the uplands, and, by choosing his routes, could wander for miles, slinging stones as he went, without risk of discovery. Whether during these months he saw any human beings is unknown; certainly no human being recognized him. His power of self-concealment amounted to genius.

Such was the second madness of Shepherd Toller. Things from the abyss of Time that float upwards into dreams—sleeping things whose breath sometimes breaks the surface of our waking consciousness, like bubbles rising from the depths of Lethe—these had become the sober certainties of Toller's life. The superincumbent waters had parted asunder, and the children of the deep were all astir. Toller had awakened into a past which lies beyond the graves of buried races and had joined his fathers in the morning of the world.

Towards the end of the summer Toller's health began to decline. He was attacked by fierce paroxysms of internal pain, which left him weak and helpless. The distant forays had to be abandoned; there was no more slinging of stones; he had great difficulty in obtaining food. He craved most for milk, and this he procured at considerable risk of discovery by descending before dawn into the lowlands and milking, or partially milking, one of the Perryman cows; for the animals knew his voice and were accustomed to his touch.

This was the posture of his affairs when one day he became apprised of the presence in the neighbourhood of the picnic-party aforesaid. He stalked them with care, saw the preparation of their meal, eyed the large basket carried by the grooms, and thought with longing of the tea it was sure to contain, and of the brandy that might be there also. To be possessed of one or both of these things would at that moment have satisfied the all-inclusive desire of the sick man's soul, and he thought of every possible device and contrivance by which he could get them into his hands. None promised well. At last he half resolved on the desperate plan of scaring the pleasure-seekers from their camp by bombarding the ground with stones—a plan which he remembered to have proved effective with a party of ladies on Clun Downs. But he doubted his strength for such a sustained effort, and reflected that a party which contained so many men, even if forced to retreat, would be sure to take their provender with them. While he was thus reflecting he saw the kettle hoisted on the tripod, shining and glinting in the sun. Never had Toller beheld a more tempting mark. The range was easy; his station was well hidden; and the kettle was the hated symbol of his disappointed hopes. ' "One more, and then I've done," I sez to myself'—thus he reported to Snarley Bob—'and I went back for the old sling, feelin' better than I'd done for weeks. I picks the best stone I could find, and kep' on whirlin' her round my head all the way back. Then I slaps her in, and blessed if I didn't take the kettle first shot!'

On the evening of the day when he discovered Toller, Snarley came home with a countenance of sorrow. 'I've found him, missis,' he said; 'but he's a dyin' man. Worn to a shadder, and him the biggest man in the parish. It would ha' scared you to see him. As sane as ever he was in his life. "Shepherd," he sez, "I'm starvin'. Can you get me a bit of summat as I can eat!" "What would you like?" I sez. He sez, "I want baccy and buttermilk. For God's sake, get me some buttermilk. It's the only thing as I feel 'ud keep down; and the pain's that awful it a'most tears me to shreds. And maybe you can find a pinch o' tea and a spot or two of something short." I sez, "You shall have it all this very night. But how's your head?" "Terrible heavy at the back," he sez, "but clear on the top. I've a'most done wi' slingin' and stealin'. The police is after me, and I'm too weak to dodge 'em much longer; they're bound to catch me soon. But they'll get nowt but a bag o' bones, and they'll have to be quick if they want 'em alive. Shepherd, I'm a dyin' man, and there's not a soul to stand by me or bury me." "Yes, there is," I sez; "you've got me. I'll stand by you, and bury you, too. If the police catches you, it'll be through no tellin' o' mine. You go back to your hut, and we'll keep you snug enough, and get you all the baccy and buttermilk as you wants." "Thank God!" he sez; and then the pain took him, and he fair rolled on the ground.'

'Yes, sir,' continued the widow of Snarley, 'my 'usband had been failin' for two years afore he died. But it was that affair wi' Shepherd Toller as broke what bit o' strength he'd got left. I wanted him to tell the doctor as he'd found him; but you might as well ha' tried to turn the church round as move my 'usband when once he'd made up his mind. "Nivver, Polly!" he sez. "I've given Shepherd Toller my word. Besides, he's too far gone for doctors to do him any good. He'll not last many days. And I knows a way o' sendin' him to sleep as beats all the doctors' bottles. You leave him to me."

'Well, you see, sir, I knowed very well as he were doing wrong. But then he didn't look at it that way. And he mostly knowed what he were doin', my 'usband did.

'He never missed goin' to Shepherd Toller's hut mornin' nor night. He took him buttermilk a'most every day; and oh, my word, the lies as he told about what he wanted it for! I've known him walk miles to get it. And then he'd sometimes sit up wi' him half the night tryin' to get him to sleep, rubbin' his back and his head. And the things my 'usband used to tell me about his sufferin's—oh, sir, it were somethin' awful! ... Once my 'usband asked him if he'd let him tell the doctor, and Shepherd Toller a'most went out o' his mind with fright. "I've got to see it through, Polly," he sez to me; "but I doubt if it won't be the death o' me."

'Shepherd Toller took to his bed the very day as my 'usband met him, and never left it, leastways he never went outside the hut again. I wanted to go myself and look after him a bit in the daytime. But my 'usband wouldn't let me go. "He's no sight for you to look at, missis," he sez. "Except for the pain, his mind's at rest. Besides there's nobody but me knows how to talk to him, and there's nobody but me as he wants to see. You can't make him no comfortabler than he is."

'But it were a terrible strain on my poor 'usband, and there's not a doubt that it would ha' killed him there and then if it had lasted much longer. It were about three weeks before the end come, and nivver shall I forget that night—no, not if I was to live to be a thousand years old.

'My master come home about ten o'clock, lookin' just like a man as were walkin' in his sleep. I couldn't get him to take notice o' nothin', and when I put his supper on the table he seemed as though he hardly knowed what it were for. He didn't eat more than two mouthfuls, and then he turned his chair round to the fire, tremblin' all over.

'After a bit I sees him drop asleep like. So I sez to myself, "I'll just go upstairs to warm his bed for him, and then I'll come down and wake him up," and I begins to get the warmin'-pan ready. He were mutterin' all sorts of things; but I didn't take much notice o' that, because that's what he allus did when he went to sleep in his chair. However, I did notice that he kep' mutterin' something about a dog.

'Soon he wakes up, kind o' startled, and sez, "Missis, let that dog in; he won't let me get a wink o' sleep." "You silly man," I sez, "you've been fast asleep for three-quarters of a' hour." "Why," he sez, "I've been wide awake all the time, listenin' to the dog whinin' and scratchin' at the door, and I was too tired to get up and let him in. Open the door quick; I'm fair sick on it." I sez, "What nonsense you're talkin'! Why, Boxer's been lyin' under the table ever since you come home at ten o'clock. He's there now." So he looks under the table, and there sure enough were Boxer fast asleep. "Well," he sez, "it must be another dog. Open the door, as I tell you, and see what it is." So I opens the door; and, of course, there were no sign of a dog. "Are you satisfied now?" I sez. "I can't make it out," he sez; "it's something funny. I'd take my dyin' oath as there were a dog scratchin'. But maybe as I'll go to sleep now." So he shuts his eyes, and were soon off, mutterin' as before.

'Well, I was just goin' upstairs when all of a sudden he give a scream as a'most made me drop the warmin' pan. "What's up?" I sez. "I've burnt my hand awful," he sez. "Burnt your hand?" I sez. "How did you manage to do that? Have you been tumblin' into the fire?" "I don't know," he sez; "but the funny thing is there's no mark of burnin' as I can see." "Why," I sez, "it must be the rheumatiz in yer knuckles. I'll get a drop o' turpentine, and rub 'em." So I gets the turpentine, and begins rubbin' his hand, and his arm as well. He sez, "It's just like a red-hot nail driven slap through the palm o' my hand." Well, it got better after a bit, and I made him go to bed, though he were that hot and excited I knowed we were going to have a wild night.

'The minute he lay down he went to sleep and slep' quietly for about half an hour. Then he starts groanin' and tossin'. "It's beginnin'," I sez to myself; "I'd better light the candle so as to be ready." The minute I struck the match he jumps out o' bed like a madman, catches hold of the bedpost, and begins pullin' the bed across the room. "What are you doin'?" I sez. "I'm pullin' the bed out o' the fire," he sez. "Don't you see the room's burnin'?" "Come, master," I sez, "you've got the nightmare. Get back into bed again, and keep quiet."

'He left go o' the bedpost and began starin' in front of him with the most awful eyes you ever see. "Are you blind?" he sez. "Don't you see what's 'appenin'?" "Nothing's 'appenin'," I sez; "get back into bed." "Look!" he sez, "look at the top o' that hill! Can't you see they're crucifying Shepherd Toller on a red-hot cross? I can hear him screamin' wi' pain." "Get out," I sez; "Shepherd Toller's all right. Now just you lie down, and think no more about it." But, oh dear, you might as well ha' talked to thunder and lightnin'. He kep' on as how he could hear Shepherd Toller screamin' and callin' for him, until I thought I should ha' gone out o' my mind.

'Just then a' idea come to me. We'd got a bottle o' stuff as the doctor give him to make him sleep when the rheumatiz come on bad. So I pours out half a cupful, and I sez, "Here, you drink that, and it'll stop 'em crucifying Shepherd Toller." He drinks it down at a gulp, and then he sez, "They've took him down. But I'm afraid he's terrible burnt." He soon got quiet and lay down and went to sleep.

'He must ha' slep' till six in the mornin', when he got up. "My head's achin' awful," he sez. "I've been dreamin' about Shepherd Toller all night. I believe as summat's gone wrong wi' him. Make me a cup o' strong tea, and I'll go and see what's up."

*

'When my 'usband got to the hut the first thing he sees were Shepherd Toller lyin' all of a heap on the floor wi' his clothes half burnt off him and his left arm lyin' right on the top o' where the fire had been. His hand were like a cinder, and he were burnt all over his body. He were still livin' and able to speak. "How's this happened—what have you been doin'?" sez my 'usband. "It were the cold," he sez, "and I wanted a drop o' brandy. And the dog were tryin' to get in. You shut him out when you went away."

'Well, my 'usband gave him brandy and managed to lift him on to the bed. "I never thought as I should die like this," he sez. "Bury the old dog wi' me, shepherd, and put the slings alongside o' me and the little axe in my hand. And see there's plenty o' stones." That was the last he said, though he kep' repeatin' it as long as he could speak. It were not more than an hour after my master found him before he were gone.

'My 'usband dug his grave wi' his own hands, close beside the hut, and buried him next day. He put the axe and slings just as he' told him, wi' the stones and all the bits of flint things as he found in the hut. What went most to his heart were shootin' the old dog. He told me as he were sure the dog knowed he were goin' to kill him, and stood as quiet as a lamb beside the grave when he pointed the gun. "It were worse than murder," he said, "and I shall see him to my dyin' day. But I'd given my word, and I had to do it."

'No, sir, not a livin' soul, exceptin' me, knew what had happened till my 'usband told Mrs Abel and you three days afore he died. That were eighteen months after he'd buried Shepherd Toller. Of course, he'd ha' got into trouble if they'd knowed what he'd done. But he weren't afraid, and he used to say to me, "Don't you bother, missis. They can't do nothing to you when I'm gone. Let 'em say what they like; you and me knows as I've done no wrong. There's only one thing as I can't bear to think on. And that's shootin' the old dog." '

SNARLEY BOB'S INVISIBLE COMPANION

WHETHER Snarley Bob was mad or sane is a question which the reader, ere now, has probably answered for himself. If he thinks him mad, his conclusion will repeat the view held, during his lifetime, by many of Snarley's equals and by some of his betters. In support of the opposite opinion, I will only say that he was sane enough to hold his tongue in general about certain matters, which, had he freely talked of them, would have been regarded as strong evidence of insanity.

The chief of these was his intercourse with the Invisible Companion—invisible to all save Snarley Bob. That designation, however, is not Snarley's, but my own; and I use it because I do not wish to commit myself to the identification of this personage with any individual, historical or imaginary. Snarley generally called him 'the Shepherd'; sometimes, 'the Master'; and he used no other name.

With this 'Master' Snarley claimed to be on terms of intimacy which go beyond the utmost reaches of authentic mysticism. Whether the being in question was a figment of the brain or a real inhabitant of time and space, let the reader, once more, decide for himself. Some being there was, at all events, of whose companionship Snarley was aware under circumstances which are not usually associated with such matters.

There is much in this connection that must needs remain obscure. The only witness who could have cleared those obscurities away has long been beyond the reach of summons. To none else than Mrs Abel was Snarley ever known to open free communication on the subject.

He spoke now and then of a dim, far-off time when he had been a 'Methody'. But he had shown scant perseverance in the road which, strait and narrow though it be, has now become easy to trace, being well marked by the tread of countless bleeding feet. Instead of continuing therein, he had 'leapt over the wall' into the surrounding waste, and struck out, by a path of his own devising, for the land of Beulah. By all recognized precedent he ought to have failed in arriving. I will not say he succeeded; but he himself was well content with the result. It is true that in all his desert-wanderings he never lost the chart and compass with which Methodism had once provided him; but he filled in the chart at points where Methodism had left it blank, and put the compass to uses which were not contemplated by the original makers.

For many years before his death Snarley entered neither the church nor the chapel; and, I regret to say, he had a very low opinion of both. This was one of the few matters on which he and Hankin were agreed, though for opposite reasons. Hankin objected to these institutions because they went too far; Snarley because they went not nearly far enough. It may, however, be noted that in the tap-room of the Nag's Head, where the blasphemy of the Divine name was a normal occurrence, Snarley, of whose displeasure everybody went in fear, would never allow the name of Christ to be so much as mentioned, not even argumentatively by Hankin; and once when a foul-mouthed navvy had used the name as part of some filthy oath, Snarley instantly challenged the man to fight, struck him a fearful blow between the eyes and pitched him headlong, with a shattered face, into the village street. But in the matter of contempt for the religious practice of his neighbours, his attitude was, if possible, more extreme than Hankin's. I need not quote his utterances on these matters; except for their unusual violence, they were sufficiently commonplace. Had Snarley been more highly developed as 'a social being' he would, no doubt, have been less intolerant; but solitude had made him blind on that side of his nature; for his fellow-men in general he had little sympathy and less admiration, his soul being as lonely as his body when wandering before the dawn on some upland waste.

Lonely, save for the frequent presence, by day and night, of his ghostly monitor and friend. To understand the nature of this companionship we must remember that devotion to the shepherd's craft was the controlling principle of Snarley's being. Had he been able to philosophize on the basis of his experience, he would have found it impossible to represent perfection as grounded otherwise than on a supreme skill in the breeding and management of sheep. No being, in his view of things, could wear the title of 'good Shepherd' for any other reason. Taking Snarley all round, I dare say he was not a bad man; but I doubt if there was any sin which smelt so rank in his nostrils as the loss of a lamb through carelessness, nor any virtue he rated so high as that which was rewarded by a first prize at the agricultural show. The form of his ideal, and the direction of his hero-worship, were determined accordingly.

The name preferred by Snarley was, as I have said, 'the Shepherd', and the term was no metaphor. He was familiar with every passage in the New Testament where mention is made of sheep; he knew, for example, the opening verses of the tenth chapter of St John by heart; and all these metaphorical passages were translated by him into literal meaning. That is to say, the Person to whom they refer, or by whom they were spoken, was one whom Snarley found it especially fitting to consult, and whose sympathy he was most vividly aware of, in doing his own duty as a guardian of sheep.

For instance, it was his practice to guide the flock by walking *before* them; and this he explained as 'a way "the Shepherd" had'. He said that when walking behind he was invariably alone; but when going in front, 'the Shepherd' was frequently by his side. And there were greater 'revelations' than this. During the lambing season, when Snarley would often spend the night in his box, high up among the wolds, 'the Shepherd' would announce his presence towards mid-night by giving a signal, which Snarley would immediately answer, and pass long hours with him communing on the mysteries of their craft.

From this source Snarley professed to have derived some of the secrets on which his system of breeding was founded. ' "The Shepherd" had put him up to them.' He said that it was 'the Shepherd' who had turned his thoughts to Spain as the country which would provide him with a short-eared ram. 'The Shepherd' had assisted in the creation of 'Thunderbolt', had indicated the meadows where the 'Spanish cross' would find the best pasturage, and never failed to warn him when he was going to make a serious mistake. In his brilliant successes, which were many, at agricultural shows and such like, Snarley disclaimed every tittle of merit for himself, assuring Mrs Abel that it was all due to the guidance of 'the Shepherd'. Of the prize-money which came to him in this way—for Farmer Perryman let him have it all—Snarley would never spend a sixpence; it was all 'the Shepherd's money', and was promptly banked 'that the missis might have a bit when he were gone'—the 'bit' amounting, if I remember rightly, to four hundred and eighty pounds.

Throughout these communings there was scarcely a trace of moral reference in the usual senses of the term. One rule of life, and one only, Snarley professed to have derived from his invisible monitor—that 'the good shepherd giveth his life for the sheep'. This rule, also, he accepted in a strictly literal sense, and considered himself under orders accordingly. Thus interpreted, it was for him the one rule which summed up the essential content of the whole moral law.

I am not able to recall any notable act of heroism or self-sacrifice performed by Snarley on behalf of his flock; but perhaps we shall not err in regarding his whole life as such an act. When, in his old age, physical suffering overtook him— the result of a life-time of toil and exposure to the elements—he bore it as a good soldier should bear his wounds, sustained by the consciousness that pain such as his was the lot of every shepherd 'as did his duty by the sheep'.

Nor am I aware that he displayed any emotional tenderness towards his charges; and certainly, I may add, his personal appearance would not have recommended him to a painter in search of a model for the Good Shepherd of traditional art. In eliminating undesirable specimens from the flock, Snarley was as ruthless as Nature; and when the butcher's man drove them off to the shambles he would watch their departure without a qualm. It was certainly said that he would never slaughter a sheep with his own hands, not even when death was merciful; on the other hand, he would sternly execute, by shooting, any dog that showed a tendency to bite or worry the flock. There was one doubtful case of this kind which Snarley told Mrs Abel he had settled by reference to his monitor—the verdict being adverse to the dog. The monitor was, indeed, his actual Master—the captain of the ship whose orders were inviolable,—Farmer Perryman being only the purser from whom he received his pay: a view of the relationship which probably worked to Perryman's great advantage.

In short, whatever may have been Snarley's sins or virtues in other directions, 'the Shepherd' had little or nothing to do with them. The burden which Snarley laid at his feet was the burden which had bent his back, and crippled his limbs, and gnarled his hands, and furrowed his broad brows during seventy years of hardship and toil. Moral lapses—in the matter of drink and, at one time, of fighting—occasionally took place; but they were never known to be followed by any reference to the disapproval of 'the Shepherd'. In some respects, indeed, Robert Dellanow showed himself singularly deficient in moral graces. To the very end of his life he was given to outbreaks of violent behaviour—as we have seen; and not only would he show no signs of after-contrition for his bad conduct, but would hint, at times, that his invisible companion had been a partner, or at least an unreproving spectator, in what he had done. But if he made a mistake in feeding the ewes or in doctoring the lambs, Snarley would say, 'I don't know what "the Shepherd" will think o' me. I'll hardly have the face to meet him next time.' Once, on the other hand, when there had been a heavy snowfall towards the end of April, and desperate work in digging the flock out of a drift, he described the success of the operations to Mrs Abel by saying, 'It were a job as "the Shepherd" himself might be proud on.'

In the last period of his life, however, gleams of his earlier Methodism occasionally shot through, and showed plainly enough of whom he was thinking. As with most men of his craft, his old age was made grievous by rheumatism; there were times, indeed, when every joint of his body was in agony. All this Snarley bore with heroic fortitude, sticking to his duties on days when he described himself as 'a'most blind wi' pain'. We have seen what sustained him, and it was strengthened, of course, as he told some of us, by the belief that 'the Shepherd' had borne far worse. When at last the rheumatism invaded the valves of his heart, and every walk up the hill was an invitation to Death, the old man still held on, unmoved by the doctor's warnings and the urgency of his friends. The Perrymans implored him to desist, and promised a pension; his wife threatened and wept; Mrs Abel added her entreaties. To the latter he replied, 'Not till I drops! As long as "the Shepherd" 's there to meet me I know as I'm wanted. The lambs ha' got to be fed. Besides, "the Shepherd" and me has an understandin'. I'll never give in while I can stand on my legs and hold my crook in my hand.'

There is reason to believe that every phase of Snarley's connection with Toller was laid before 'the Shepherd'. Each new development was subject to his guidance. Shortly after Toller's disappearance, Snarley said to Mrs Abel, 'Me and "the Shepherd" has been talkin' it over. He sez to me, "Snarley, when you lose a sheep, you goes after it into the wilderness, and you looks and looks till you finds it. But this time it's a shepherd that's lost. Now you stay quiet where you are, and keep your eyes and ears open day and night. I know where he is; he's all right; and I'm lookin' after him. By and by I'm going to hand him over to you. Him and you has got to drink together, but it'll be a drink o' gall for both on you. When the time comes, I'll give you the sign." '

'The sign come,' he added, later on, 'the sign come that night in the Nag's Head, when the groom told us about the kettle. I'd just had a drop o' something short, and when I looks up there were "the Shepherd" sittin' in the chair next but one to Shoemaker Hankin. Just then the groom come in, and "the Shepherd" gets up and comes over to a little table where I'd got my glass. The groom sits down where "the Shepherd" had been, and "the Shepherd" sits down opposite to me. The groom says,

"Boys, I've got summat to tell you as'll make your hair stand on end." "Fire away," says Tom Barter; and "the Shepherd", he holds up his finger and looks at me. When the groom had done, and they were all shoutin' and laughin', "the Shepherd" leans across the table and whispers, close in my ear, "Snarley, the hour's come! Drink up what's left in your glass. It's time to be goin'.'

During the trying time of his concealment and tending of Toller, 'the Shepherd' 's presence became more frequent, and Snarley's characterization more precise. The belief that 'the Shepherd' was 'backing him up' gave Snarley a will of iron. When Mrs Abel, on the night of his confession, essayed to reprove him for not obtaining medical assistance for Toller, he drew himself as erect as his crippled limbs allowed, and said quietly, in a manner that closed discussion, 'It were "the Master's" orders, my lady. He'd handed him over to *me*.' He also said, or hinted, that 'the Master' had taught him the method—whatever it may have been—for sending Toller to sleep, 'that were better than all the doctor's bottles.' From the same source, doubtless, came his secret for 'setting Toller's mind at rest'. That secret is undivulged; but it was connected in some way with what Snarley called 'the Shepherd's Plan', of which all we could learn was that 'there were three men on three crosses, him in the middle being "the Shepherd", and them at the sides being Toller and me'.

'There were allus three on us in the hut,' said Snarley, 'and all three were men as knowed what pain were. Both Toller and me was drinking out o' "the Shepherd's" cup, and he'd promised to stay by us till the last drop was gone. "It's full o' fury and wrath," sez he; "but it's got to be drunk by them as wants to drive their flock among the stars. I've gone before, and you're comin' after. When you've done this there'll be no more like it. The next cup will be full o' wine, and we'll all three drink it together." '

In this wise did Snarley and Toller receive the Sacrament in their dark and lonely den.

The night on which Snarley came home 'like a man walking

in his sleep'—the last night of Toller's life—was wild, wet, and very dark. With a lantern in one hand, a can of milk in the other, and a bag of sticks on his back, the old man stumbled through the night until he reached the last slope leading to Toller's hut. Here the lantern was blown out, and Snarley, after depositing his burdens, sat down, dizzy and faint, on a stone. In his pocket was an eight-ounce bottle containing a meagre six-penn'orth of brandy for Shepherd Toller. Snarley fingered the bottle, and then, with quick resolution, withdrew his hand. 'For the life o' me,' he said, 'I couldn't remember where I was. I felt as though the hillside were whirlin' round, carryin' me with it. And then I felt as though I were sinkin' into the ground. "I'll never get there this night," I sez to myself. Just then I hears something movin', and blessed if it wasn't Toller's old dog as had come to look for me. He come jumpin' up and begins lickin' my face. Well, it put a bit o' heart into me to feel the old dog. So I picks up the can and the bundle, and off I goes again; and, though I wouldn't ha' believed it, it weren't more than eighty yards, or a hundred at most, to the hut.

'When I come to the edge of the pit I sees a lantern burnin' near the door, wonderful bright; and there were "the Shepherd" sittin' on a stone, same as I'd been doin' myself a minute before. As soon as he sees me comin', he waves his lantern and calls out, "Have a care, Snarley, it's a steep and narrow road." Well, the path down into the pit were as slippery as ice, and I tell you I'd never ha' got down—at least, not without breakin' some o' my bones—if "the Shepherd" hadn't kep' showin' me a light.

'So I comes up to where he were; and then I noticed as he were wet through, just as I were, and looking regular wore out. "Snarley," he sez to me, "you carry your cross like a man." "I learnt that from you, Master," I sez; "but you look as though yours had been a bit too heavy for you this time." "We've had terrible work to-day," he sez; "we've been dividin' the sheep from the goats. And there's no keepin' 'em apart. We no sooner gets 'em sorted than they mixes themselves up again, till you don't know where you are." "Why didn't you let me come and help you?" I sez. "I'd ha' brought Boxer, and he'd ha' settled 'em pretty quick." "No, no," he sez; "your hour's not come. When I wants you, I'll give you a sign as you can't mistake. Besides, you're not knowledgable in goats. Feed my sheep." "Well," I sez, "when you wants me, you knows where to find me." "Right," he sez; "but it's Toller we'll be wantin' first. And I've been thinkin' as p'raps he'd oblige us by lettin' us have the loan of his dog for a bit." "I'll go in and ask him," I sez; "I don't suppose he'll have any objection." Then "the Shepherd" blew his lantern out, and I see him no more that night.

'Me and the dog goes into the hut, and I could hear as Toller were fast asleep in his bed. I begins blowin' up the embers in the fire, and when the blaze come the old dog lay down as though he meant goin' to sleep. But I could see as there was somethin' on his mind, for he kept cockin' his nose up, and sniffin' and lookin' round. Then he gets up and begins scratchin' at the door, as he allus did when he wanted to go out. So I opens the door, and out he rushes into the dark, like a mad thing, barkin' as though he smelt a fox.

'When I'd done what I'd come to do, I puts the brandy and the buttermilk where they'd be handy for Shepherd Toller to get 'em, and then I goes to the door and begins whistlin' for the dog. But no sign of him could I hear or see, though I kep' on whistlin' for a full a quarter of a' hour. It were strange as it didn't wake Shepherd Toller, but he kep' on sleepin' like a child in a thunderstorm. At last I give it up and shut the door and went home. How I got back, I don't know. I can't remember nothing till my missis catched hold on me and pulled me in through the door.'

*

'I'd never ha' been able to shoot the old dog,' said Snarley, 'if "the Shepherd" hadn't made me do it. I turned fair sick when I put the charge in the gun, and when I pointed it at him I was in such a tremble that I couldn't aim straight. I tried three or four times to get steady, the dog standin' as still as still all the while, except that he kep' waggin' his tail.

'All of a sudden I sees "the Shepherd", plain as plain. He were standin' just behind the old dog, strokin' his head. "Shoot, Snarley," he sez; "shoot, and we'll look after him." "Stand back, then, Master," I sez; "for I'm goin' to fire." "Fire," he sez; "but aim lower. The shot won't hurt *me*," and he went on strokin' the dog's head. So I pulls the trigger, and when the smoke cleared "the Shepherd" were gone, and the dog were lyin' dead as any stone.'

THE DEATH OF SNARLEY BOB

'HE'D a rough tongue, sir; but he'd a good 'eart,' said the widow of Snarley Bob. 'Oh, sir, but he were a wonderful man, were my master. I never knowed one like him—no, nor never 'eard o' one. I didn't think on it while he were living; but now he's gone I know what I've lost. That clever! Why, he often used to say to me, "Polly, there ain't a bit of blessed owt as I couldn't do, if I tried." And it were true, sir. And him nothing but a shepherd all his life, and never earned more'n eighteen shillin' a week takin' it all the year round. And us wi' a family of thirteen children, without buryin' one on 'em, and all married and doin' well. And only one fault, sir, and that not so bad as it is in some. He *would* have his drop of drink—that is, whenever he could get it. Not that he spent his wages on it, except now and then after the children was growed up. But you see, sir, he was that amusin' in his talk, and folks used to treat him.

'Well, sir, it was last Saturday fortnight, as I was tellin' you, he come home for the last time. I can see 'im now, just as he come staggerin' in at that door. I thought when I saw him that he'd had a drop o' drink, though he'd not been 'avin' any for a long time. So I sez to myself, "I'd better make 'im a cup o' tea," and I begins puttin' the kettle on the fire. "What are you doin'?" he sez. "I'm goin' to give you a cup o' tea," I sez; "it'll do yer good." "No, it won't," he sez, "I've done wi' cups o' tea in this world." "Why," I sez, "what rubbish! 'Ere, sit yer down, and let me pull yer boots off." "You can pull 'em off," he sez, "but ye'll never see me put 'em on again."

'I could see by this that it wasn't drink, besides I couldn't smell any. So I gets 'im into his chair and begins pullin' his boots off. "What makes you talk like that?" I sez. "You knows as you was ever so much better last night. When you've had yer medicine you'll be all right." He said nowt for a time, but just sat, tremblin' and shiverin' in his chair. So I sez, "Hadn't you better 'ave the doctor?" "It's no good," he sez; "I'm come 'ome for the last time. It'll be good-bye this time, missis." "Not it," I sez, "you've got many years to live yet. Why, wot's to make yer die?" "It's my 'eart," he sez; "it's all flip-floppin' about inside me, and gurglin' like a stuck pig. It's wore out, and I keep gettin' that faint." "Oh," I sez, "cheer up; when you've 'ad a cup o' tea you'll feel better"; but I'd hardly got the words out o' my mouth before he were gone in a dead faint.

*

'We got 'im to bed between the three on us, and, my word, it were a job gettin' 'im up them narrer stairs! As soon as we'd made 'im comfortable, he sez to me, "Wot I told yer's coming tonight, Polly. They've been a-callin' on me all day. I see 'em and 'ear 'em, too. Loud as loud. Plain as plain." "Who's been callin' yer?" I sez. "The messengers o' death," he sez; "and they're in this room, four on 'em, now. I can 'ear 'em movin' and talkin' to one another." "Oh," I sez, "it's all fancy. What you 'ear is me and Mrs Rowe. You lie quiet and go to sleep, and you'll be better in the mornin'." He only shook his 'ead and said, "I can 'ear 'em."

'Well, I suppose it was about 'alf a' hour after this when Mrs Rowe sez to me, "He looks like goin' to sleep now, Mrs Dellanow, so I think I'll go 'ome and get my master 'is supper"; and she was just goin' down the stairs when all of a sudden he starts up in bed and sez, "Do you 'ear that whistle blowin'?" "No," I sez, "you've been dreamin'. There isn't nobody whistlin' at this time o' night." "Yes," he sez, "there is, and it blowed three times. There's thousands and thousands of sheep, and a tall shepherd whistlin' to his dog. But he's got no dog, and it's me he's whistlin' for."

'Now, sir, you must understand that my 'usband when he was with the sheep used to work his dog wi' whistlin' instead of shoutin' to it as most shepherds do. You can see his whistle hangin' on that nail—that's where he hung it 'isself for twenty-five years. You see, he was kind o' superstitious and used to say

it was bad luck to keep yer whistle in yer pocket when you went
to bed. So he always hung it on that nail, the last thing at night.

' "Why," I sez, tryin' to humour 'im, "it's his dog he's whistlin' for, not you. His dog's somewhere where you can't see it.
He doesn't want you. You lie back again, and go to sleep." "No,
no," sez he; "there's no dog, and the sheep's runnin' everywhere, thousands on 'em. It's me he's whistlin' for, and we must
whistle back to say I'm comin'. Fetch it down from the nail,
Polly. There he is again! He's the tallest shepherd I ever saw.
He's one of them four that was in the room just now. Whistle
back, Polly, and then it'll be all right." And so he kep' on, again
and again.

'Mrs Rowe, who'd come into the room, said to me, "If I was
you, Mrs Dellanow, I'd fetch the whistle and blow it. It'll quiet
'im, and then p'raps he'll go to sleep."

'You can understand, sir, that I was that upset I didn't know
what I was doing. But when he kep' on callin' and beseechin' I
thought I'd better do as Mrs Rowe recommended. So I went
down and took the whistle from that nail—the same where you
see it hangin' now. When I got back I couldn't somehow bring
myself to do it, so I gives it to 'im to blow 'isself. But, oh dear, to
see the poor thing trying to put it to his mouth ... it a'most
broke my heart. So I took it from 'im, and blowed it myself
three times as he wanted me. To think o' me standin' by my
own 'usband's dyin'-bed and blowin' a whistle!

'When I'd done, he says, "That's all right; he knows I'm
comin' now. But it'll take a long time to gather all them sheep."

'For a bit he was quite still, and both me and Mrs Rowe sat
watchin', when, all of a sudden, he starts up again and sez,
"Listen, he's goin' to blow again." Well, sir, I dare say you won't
believe what I'm going to tell yer, but it's as true as I'm standin'
'ere. He'd hardly got the words out of his mouth when I hears a
whistle blown three times—leastways I thought I did—as it
might be coming from the top of that 'ill you see over there.
There weren't no other sounds, for it was as still a night as
could be. But there was someone whistling, and Mrs Rowe
'eard it too. If you don't believe me, you can ask her. I nearly

dropped on the floor, and I knew from that minute that my 'usband was going to die.

*

'You see, sir, my 'usband was never what you might call a religious man. He were more of a readin' man, my 'usband was—papers and books and all sorts o' things—more'n was good for 'im, I often used to say. You can see a lot on 'em on that little shelf. If it hadn't been that they kep' 'im out o' the Nag's Head I'd ha' burned some on 'em, that I would, and I often told 'im so. He knowed a wonderful lot about the stars, my 'usband did. Why, he'd often sit in his chair outside that door, smokin' his pipe and watchin' 'em for hours together.

'One day there was a great man came down to give a lecture on the stars in C——, and a gentleman as knowed my 'usband's tastes paid his fare and gave 'im a ticket for the lecture. When he came 'ome he was that excited I thought he'd go out o' his mind. He seemed as though he could think of nothing else for weeks, and it wasn't till he began to ha' bad luck wi' the ewes as he was able to shake it off. He was allus lookin' in the paper to see if the gentleman as give the lecture was comin' again. His name was Sir Robert Ball. I dare say you've heard on 'im.

'He used to spend all his Sundays readin' about stars. No, sir he 'adn't been inside the church for years. "Church is for folks as knows nowt about the stars," he used to say. "Sir Robert Ball's my parson." One night when he was sittin' outside the door, I sez, "Why don't you come in and get yer supper? It's getting cold." "Let it get cold," he sez; "I'm not comin' in till the moon's riz. It's as good as a drop o' drink to see it."

'P'raps he told yer all about that time when he was took up wi' spiritualism. He'd met a man in the public-'ouse who'd 'eard his talk and put 'im up to it. They got 'im to go to a meetin' i' the next village, and made 'im believe as he was a medium. Well, there never was such goin's-on as we 'ad wi' 'im for months. He'd sit up 'alf the night, bumpin' the table and tan-rannin' wi' an old bucket till I was a'most scared out o' my life. But that winter he was nearly carried off wi' the New Mony, and when he got better he said he wasn't goin' to touch the spirits no more. "There's summat in it," he sez; "but there's more in the stars." And from that day I never 'eard 'im so much as talk about spirits, and you may be sure I didn't remind 'im on 'em.

'You must ha' often 'eard 'im talk about the stars, sir. Well, I suppose them things makes no difference to a' eddicated gentleman like you. But poor folks, *I* sez, has no business to meddle wi' 'em. All about worlds and worlds floatin' on nothin' till you got fair lost. Folks as find them things out ought to keep 'em quiet, that's wot *I* sez. Why, I've 'eard 'im talk till I was that mazed that I couldn't 'a said my prayers; no, not if I'd tried ever so.

*

'Yes, sir, it were a strange thing that when my 'usband come to die his mind seemed to hang on his whistle more'n a'most anything else. He kep' talkin' about it all night, and sayin' the tall shepherd was answerin' back, though I never 'eard nothin' myself, save that one time I told yer of.

' "It's queer he don't talk about the stars," sez Mrs Rowe to me. "He will do before he's done, you see if he doesn't," I sez.

'Well, about three o'clock I see a change in his face and knowed as the end wasn't far off. So I puts my arm round his old neck, and I sez, "Bob, my dear, are you prepared to meet your Maker?" "Oh! I'm all right," he sez quite sensible; "don't you bother your head about that." "Don't you think you'd better let me send for the parson?" I sez. "No," he sez; "but you could send for Sir Robert Ball—if you only knew where to find him." "But," I sez, "wouldn't you like somebody to pray with yer? Sir Robert Ball's no good for that." "He's as good as anybody else," he sez. "Besides what's the use of prayin' now? It's all over." "It might do yer good," I sez. "It's too late," he sez, "and I don't want it. It isn't no Maker I'm goin' to—I'm goin' to the stars." "Oh," I sez, "you're dreamin' again." "No, I'm not," he sez. "Didn't I tell yer they'd been a-callin' on me all day? I don't mean the stars, but them as lives in 'em."

'No, sir, he wasn't wanderin' then. "I wish the children was 'ere," he sez; "but you couldn't get 'em all in this little room. My eye, what a lot we've 'ad! And all livin'. And there's Tom got seven of 'is own." And a lot more like that; but I was so upset and crying that I can't remember half on it.

'About four o'clock he seemed to rally a bit and asked me to put my arm round him and lift him up. So I raises him, like, on the pillow and gives him a sup o' water. "What day o' the week is it?" he sez. "Sunday mornin'," I sez. "That's my day for the stars," he sez, and a smile come over his face, as were beautiful to see ... No, sir, he weren't a smilin' man, as a rule—he allus got too much on his mind—and a lot o' pain to bear too, sir. Oh, dear me! ... Well, as I was a-sayin', he were as glad as glad when he heard it were Sunday. "What's o'clock?" he sez. "Just struck four by the church clock," I sez. "Then the dawn must be breakin'," he sez; "look out o' the winder, there's a good lass, and tell me if the sky's clear, and if you can see the mornin' star in the south-east." So I goes to the winder and tells him as how the sky were clear and the mornin' star shinin' wonderful. "Ah, she's a beauty," he sez, "and as bright as she were millions o' years ago!"

'After a bit he sez, "Take yer arm off, Polly, and lay me on my right side." When me and Mrs Rowe 'ad turned 'im round he sez, "You can fetch the old Bible and read a bit if you like." "What shall I read?" I sez, when Mrs Rowe had fetched it, for I wouldn't leave 'im for a minute. "Read about the Woman in Adultery," he sez. "Oh," I sez, "that'll do you no good. You don't want to 'ear about them things now." "Yes," he sez, "I do. It's the best bit in the book. But if you can't find it, the Box o' Hointment'll do as well." "What can he mean?" I sez. "He means about them two women as come to our Lord," sez Mrs Rowe. " 'Ere, I'll find 'em." So I give the Bible to Mrs Rowe and lets her read both of the bits he wanted.

'While Mrs Rowe was readin' he lay as still as still, but his eyes were that bright it a'most scared me to see 'em. When she'd done, he said never a word, but lay on 'is side, wi' 'is 'ead turned a bit round, starin' at the window. "I'm sure he sees summat," sez Mrs Rowe to me. "I wonder wot it is," I sez. "P'raps it's our Lord come to fetch 'im," she sez. "I've 'eard o' such things."

'He must ha' lay like that for ten minutes, breathin' big breaths as though he were goin' to sleep. Then I sees 'is lips movin', and I 'ad to bend my 'ead down to 'ear what he were sayin'. "He's a-blowin' again. It's the tall shepherd—'im as wrote on the ground—and he's got no dog, and 'is sheep's scatterin'. It's me he wants. Fetch the old whistle, Polly, and blow back. I want 'im to know I'm comin'."

*

'He kep' repeatin' till 'is breath went. I got Mrs Rowe to blow the whistle, but he didn't 'ear it, and it made no difference. And so, poor thing, he just gave one big sigh and he were gone.'

Other Human Studies

*

FARMER PERRYMAN'S TALL HAT

IT was winter, and Farmer Perryman and I were seated in straight-backed arm-chairs on either side of his kitchen fire. The prosperity attendant on the labours of Snarley Bob had already begun: the house was roomy and well furnished; there was a parlour and a drawing-room; but Perryman, when the day's work was done, preferred the kitchen. And so did I.

Though evening had fallen, the lamp was not yet lit; but the flames of a wood fire gave light enough for conversational purposes, and imparted to the flitches and hams suspended from the ceiling a lively reality which neither daylight nor petroleum could ever produce. As the shadows danced among them, the kitchen became peopled with friendly presences; a new fragrance pervaded the place, bearing a hint of good things to come. No wonder that Perryman loved the spot.

To-night, however, there was another object in the room, of so alien a nature that any self-respecting ham or flitch, had it possessed a reasonable soul, would have been sorely tempted to 'heave half a brick' at the intruder. This object stood gleaming on a table in the middle of the room. It was a bran-new and brilliantly polished tall hat.

'No,' said Farmer Perryman, 'it's not for Sundays. It's for a weddin'! You'll never see me wearing a box-hat on Sundays again. Will he, missis?' (Mrs Perryman said, 'I don't expect he will.') 'No sir, not again! Not that I don't mean to go to church regular. I've done that all my life.

'Yes, you're quite right. Folks in the villages don't go to church as they used to do when I was a young man, and I'm sorry to see it. Folks nowadays seems to have forgotten as

they've got to die. Besides, it's not good for farmin'. Show me
any parish in the county where there's first-class farmin', and
I'll bet you three to one there's a good congregation in the
church.

'What's driven 'em away, did you say? Well, if you want my
opinion, it's my belief as this 'ere Church Restoration has as
much to do wi' it as anything else. There's been a lot o' new
doctrine, it's true, and all this 'ere 'Igh Churchism, as I could
never make head nor tail of; and that, no doubt, has offended
some o' the old-fashioned folk like me. But it's when they starts
restoring the old churches, and makin' 'em all spick and span,
that the religious feelin' seems to die out on 'em, and folks
begins to stop goin'. You might as well be in a concert hall—
the place full o' chairs and smellin' o' varnish enough to make
you sick, and a lot o' lads in the chancel dressed up in white
gowns, and suckin' sweets, and chuckin' paper pellets at one
another all through the sermon. That's not what *I* call religion!

'I've often told our parson as it were the worst day's work he
ever did when he had our church restored. And a lot o' money
it cost, too; but not a penny would I give, and I told 'em I
wouldn't—no, not if they'd gone down on their bended knees.
From that day to this our church has never *smelt* right—never
smelt as a church *ought* to smell. You know the smell of a' old
church? Well, I don't know what makes it; but there it is, and
when you've said your prayers to it for forty years you can't say
'em to no other.

'I can remember what a turn it gave me that Sunday when
the Bishop came down to open the church after it had been
restored. The old smell clean gone, and what was worse a new
smell come! "Mr Abel," I says, "I can put up wi' a bit of new
doctrine, and I don't mind a pinch or two o' ceremony; but I
can't abide these 'ere new smells." "I'll never be able to keep on
comin'," I says to Charley Shott. "Nor me, neither," he says. "I'll
go to church in another parish," I says to my missis, "for
danged if you'll ever see me goin' inside a chapel."

'So I went next Sunday to Holliton, and—would you believe
me?—it had a new smell, worse, if anything, than ours. There

was a' old man in a black gown, and a long stick in his hand, walkin' up and down the aisle. So I says to him, "What's up with this 'ere church? Has them candles on the altar been smokin'?" "No," he says, "not as I know on." "Well," I says, sniffin' like, "there's a very queer smell in the place. It's not 'ealthy. Summat ought to be done to it at once." "Hush!" he says, "what you smells is the incense." And then the Holliton clergyman! Well—I couldn't stand him at no price—a great, big, fat feller wi' no more religion in him than a cow—and not more'n six people in the church. "Not for me," I says, "not after Mr Abel."

'Well, I didn't know what to do, when one day I sees Charley Shott comin' out o' our churchyard. "Sam," he says, "I've just been sniffin' round inside the church, and there she is, all alive and kickin'!" "What's all alive and kickin'?" I says. "The old smell," says he; "come inside, and I'll show you where she is." So I follows Charley Shott into the church, and he takes me round to where the old tomb is, in the north transep'. "Now," he says, "take a whiff o' that, Sam." "Charley," I says, "it's the right smell sure enough; and if only she won't wear off, I'll sit in this corner to the end o' my days." "She's not likely to wear off," he says, "she comes from the old tomb. It's a mixture o' damp and dust. Now, the damp's all right, because the heatin' pipes don't come round here; and, besides, the sun never gets into this corner. And as to the dust, you just take your pocket-handkerchief and give a flick or two round the bottom o' the tomb. That'll freshen her up any time."

'Well, you may laugh; but I tell you it's as true as I'm sittin' here. I allus goes to church in good time, and if my corner don't smell true, I just dusts her up a bit, and then she's as right as a trivet.'

'But,' I said, 'you were going to tell me about the tall hat.'

'Ha, so I was,' replied Perryman; 'but the hat made me think o' the church, and that put me off. Well, it's no doin' o' mine that you see that hat where it is to-night. If I had my way it 'ud be in the place where it came from, and fifteen shillin's that's in another place 'ud be in my pocket. I'm not used to 'em, and what's more I never shall be. But a weddin's a weddin', and your niece is your niece, and when your missis says you've got to wear one—why, what's the use o' sayin' you won't? However, that's not the first tall hat as I've worn.'

'Tell me about the others,' I said.

'There was only one other, and that other was one "other" too many for me,' replied the farmer. 'It's seven years come next hay harvest since my wife come into a bit of money as had been left her by her aunt. "Sam," she says to me, "we got a rise, and we must act up to it." "Right you are," I says; "but how are you goin' to start?" "Well," she says, "the first thing you've got to do is to leave off wearing billy-cocks on Sundays and buy a box-hat." "Polished 'ats," I says, "is for polished 'eads, and mine was ordered plain." "If there's no polish on your 'ead," says she, "that's a reason for having some on your 'at."

'Well, we had a bit more chaff, and the end of it was that I promised to buy one, though, between you and me, I never meant to. However, when market-day come round, she *would* go with me, and never a bit of peace did she give me till she'd driven me into a shop and made me buy the hat. "I've bought it, Sally," I said; "but you'll *never* see me wear it." "Oh yes, I shall," she says; "you're not nearly such a fool as you try to make yourself out." Well, I went home that day just as mad as mad. If there's one thing in this world as upsets me it's spending money on things I don't want. And there was twelve-and-sixpence gone on a box-hat! If Sally hadn't kept hold on it I'd ha' kicked the whole thing half a mile further than the middle of next week. "I'll get that twelve-and-sixpence back somehow," I said to myself; "you see if I don't. It's the Church that made me spend it, and the Church shall pay me back. If I didn't go to church I shouldn't have bought that hat. All right, Mr Church," I said, as I drove by it, shakin' my fist at the steeple, "I'll be even with you yet"; and I shouted it out loud.'

'I should have thought your wife had more to do with it than the Church,' I interposed.

'Of course she had—in a plain sense o' speakin',' said the farmer. 'But then your wife's your wife, especially when she's a good 'un, and the Church is the Church. Some men might ha' rounded on Sally; but I told her before we were married that the first bad word I gave her would be the answer to one she gave me. That's eight-and-twenty year ago, and we haven't begun yet. But where was I? Oh, I was tellin' you what I said to the church. You can guess what a rage I was in from my gettin' such a' idea into my 'ead.'

'No other reason?' I asked.

'Not a drop,' replied Perryman; 'for I suppose that's what you mean. No, sir, I give it up once and for all ever since that time when Mrs Abel followed me to Crawley Races. Ay, and the best day's work she ever did— and that's sayin' a good deal, I can tell you. I can see her just as she was. She were drivin' a little blood-mare as she'd bought o' me—one as I'd bred myself—for I were more in 'osses than sheep in them days—and Mrs Abel were allus a lady as knowed a good 'oss when she see it. And there was Snarley Bob, in his Sunday clothes, sittin' on the seat behind. She'd got a little blue bonnet on, as suited her to a T, and were lookin' like a—'

'Tell him about that some other time,' said Mrs Perryman; 'if you go on at this rate you'll never get finished with the story about your hat.'

'Hats isn't everything,' said the farmer; 'but if hats is what you want to hear about, hats is what I'll talk on.'

Mrs Perryman looked at me with a glance which seemed to say that, even though hats weren't everything, we had better stick to them on the present occasion. I interpreted the glance by saying to the farmer, 'Go on about the hat. We can have the other next time.' Mrs Perryman seemed relieved, and her husband continued:

'Well, next mornin' bein' Sunday, the missis managed to get her way, and off we sails to church—she in a silk dress, and me in a box-hat. We was twenty minutes before time, for I didn't want people to see us; but, just as we were crossing the church-yard, who should we meet but the parson and his lady? Know our parson? You're right: he's not only good, but good all through fat, lean, and streaky. That's what he is, and you can take my word for it. Know his lady? No?' (I was a new-comer in those days.) 'Well, you *ought* to: she'd make you laugh till you choked, and next minute she'd make you cry. Mischievous? Why, if I should tell you the tricks she's played on people you wouldn't believe 'em. Ever hear what she did when the Squire's son come of age? Or about her dressing up at the Queen's Jubilee? No? Well, I'll tell you that another time. Oh, she's a treat—a real treat!' (Here Farmer Perryman broke forth into mighty laughter and banged his fist on the table with such vigour that Tall Hat the Second leaped into the air.)

'Why doesn't Parson keep her under, did you say?' he continued. 'Bless yer heart, he doesn't want to. She never harmed a living soul. Why, the good she's done to this parish couldn't be told. It'll take the whole of the Judgement Day to get through it, and then they won't ha' done—that's what folks says. Popular? I should think she *was*! There isn't a poor man or woman in the village as doesn't worship the soles of her boots. And there's not many, rich or poor, as she hasn't made fools of—yes, and more than once. They ought to write a book about her. It's a shame they don't. My eye, if she'd been Queen of England she'd ha' made things jump! As for finding things out, she's got a nose like that little terrier bitch o' mine. 'Pon my word, it wouldn't surprise me if she knows that you're sittin' in that chair at this minute. You mayn't believe me, but I tell you she's capable of more than that.

'Yes, yes, she's gettin' an old woman now. I remember the day as Parson brought her home—a quiet-looking little thing, with a face like a tame rabbit—you wouldn't ha' thought she could 'a bitten a hole in the cheek of a' apple. Some say she was a' actress before he married her; she's *clever* enough for twenty actresses, and she's *better* than twenty thousand.'

'Those are impressive figures,' I said, not a little puzzled by the sum in moral arithmetic which the farmer's enthusiasm had propounded. 'Why, she must be a perfect saint.'

The words were scarcely out of my mouth when Mr Perryman rose from his chair like a man in wrath. Inadvertently I had used an expression which acted like a spark upon gunpowder. Intending to praise his idol, I had for some obscure reason wounded the passionate old man in the most sensitive nerve of his being. I sat amazed, not understanding what I had done, and even now I do not pretend to understand it wholly. But this is what happened. Standing over me with fierce gesticulations, Mr Perryman poured out a fury of words, only fragments of which I can now recall.

'Perfect saint!' he shouted. 'Do you know who it is you're talking about? No, you don't, or you'd never have said such a word! Look here, mister, let me tell yer this: you're on the wrong side of your 'osses this time! She's no more a saint than *I* am; if she had been, do you think she could ha' done the best thing she ever did?'

'Great heavens!' I thought, 'what can he mean?—I'm sorry you're hurt,' I said aloud. 'I meant no offence. Only you said just now she was as good as twenty thousand—'

'*Actresses*,' broke in the farmer. 'I said twenty thousand actresses—not twenty thousand *lambs*.'

'Oh, well,' I replied, 'of course, there's a great difference between the two things, and I was stupid not to think of it before. Whatever she may be, it's plain you admire her, and that's enough.' I was anxious to break the current of Mr Perryman's thoughts, and recover the history of the Tall Hat, the thread of which had been so unexpectedly snapped.

'Admire her!' cried the old man, who was evidently not to be put off. 'And why shouldn't I? Who was it that dug Sam Perryman out of the mud when he was buried in it up to his neck—yes, and got half smothered with mud herself in doing it? But do you think she *cared*? Not she! Snapped her fingers in the face of half the county, that she did, and what's more she gave some of 'em a taste of the whip as they won't forget! Now listen, and I'll tell you something that'll make your hair curl.'

I swiftly resolved not to listen, for the farmer was beside himself with excitement and not responsible for what he was doing. I saw that I was about to discover what I was never intended to know. Dim recollections came to my mind of a grotesque but terrible story, known to not more than four living souls, the names and personalities in which had for good reasons been carefully concealed from me and from others. That Farmer Perryman was one actor in that tragedy, and that Mrs Abel was another, had been already revealed past recalling. More than this it was unseemly that I should hear.

The figure of the old man, as he stood before me then, is one of those images that cannot be effaced. His voice was broken, his lips were parted and quivering, his form rigid but unsteady, and the furrows on his brow ran into and crossed one another like the lines on a tragic mask. He was about to proceed, and I to protest against his doing so, when an incident occurred which relieved the tension and gave a new turn to the course of events.

Mrs Perryman, who had left the room when the farmer resumed the history of the Tall Hat, though not to go beyond the reach of hearing, now emerged from the shadows and said in a quiet voice, 'Sam, stop talking a minute, and attend to business. Snarley Bob's at the back door, and wants to know if you're going to keep him waiting all night. He come for his wages at five o'clock, and it's struck six some time ago.'

'Give him a mug o' ale, and tell him to go home,' said Sam.

'I've given him two mugs already, and he says he must see you afore he goes.'

'Wait where you are,' said Mr Perryman to me, 'and I'll be back in half a shake.'

The Perrymans withdrew together, leaving me alone. I listened to the voices in the next room and could distinguish those of the farmer and his wife, urgent but subdued. I could not hear the voice of Snarley Bob. Then I drew conclusions, and searched in the recesses of my memory for a forgotten clue. Gazing into the fire, I saw three separate strands of smoke roll themselves into a single column, and rush upwards into the darkness of the chimney. The thing acted as a stimulus to recollection, for it spoke of three human lives flowing onwards to the Unknown in a single stream of destiny: Mrs Abel, Farmer Perryman, Snarley Bob—and further articulations would have

followed had not the re-entry of the Perrymans disturbed the
process and plunged it back beneath the threshold of consciousness. The farmer's wife sat down between us, in front of
the fire.

'I want to hear him finish the story of the Tall Hat,' she said.
'With me by he's less likely to put the frilling on.'

'Let's see—where was I?' said Perryman.

'You'd come to the place where you met the parson and his
lady in the churchyard,' I said.

'Ha, so I had,' replied the farmer. 'I can see her at this very
minute just as she was. She looked—'

'Never mind what she *looked* like: tell us what she *said*,'
interrupted Mrs Perryman.

'She says, "Good-morning, Mr Perryman. How much?"
—looking 'ard at my 'at all the time. I guessed she was
up to some devilry, so I thought I would put her wrong a bit. "A
guinea, ma'am," says I. She looks at my 'at again and says, "Mr
Perryman, you've been took in. Twelve-and-six would have
been more than enough for that 'at.' "Oh," says I to myself,
"you've been nosing round already, 'ave you?" I suppose I must
have looked a bit foolish like—I'm sure I felt it,—but she didn't
give me no time to speak. "Wouldn't you like to have that
guinea back in your pocket?" says she, putting a funny sound
on the "guinea." "Yes," I says; "and, what's more, I mean to get
it back." "Oh indeed," says she, and a look come into her face as
though she was putting two and two together. After a bit
she says "Mr Perryman, was that your trap that drove by
about half-past seven last night?" "Yes," I says; and I might
have known from that minute she was going to do a down
on me.

'However, I'd made up my mind how I was goin' to get that
money back, and I wasn't goin' to change for nobody. You must
understand there's a weekly offertory in our church. There was
a lot of objection when Parson started it years ago. But, you see,
he's always been a bit 'Igh.' ('Much too High for me,' here
interposed Mrs Perryman.) 'Yes, I've warned him about it several times. "Mr Abel," I says to him, "you're 'Igh enough

already. Now, you take my advice, and don't you get no 'Igher." That was when he started the offertory.

'Well, I'm the sort of man that when I gives, I gives. Ever since the offertory was begun my missis puts a two-shillin' piece into the waistcoat-pocket of my Sunday suit— don't you, Sally?' (Sally nodded)—'regular every Monday morning when she brushes my clothes, so there's no doubt about its being there when Sunday comes. That's for collection.

'And now you can understand my plan. I'd made up to give one shillin' instead o' two, Sunday by Sunday, till I'd paid for my new box-hat. That's how I was goin' to get even with the Church.

'I kep' it up regular for twelve weeks, counting 'em off one by one. I didn't bother about the sixpence. Meanwhile two or three other farmers, not wanting to be put in the shade by me—or more likely it was their missises— had begun to wear box-hats o' Sunday. There was Tom Henderson, who's no more fit to wear a box-hat than his bull is; and there was old Charley Shott—know him?—a man with a wonderful appetite for pig-meat is old Charley Shott. It would ha' made you die o' laughin' to see old Charley come shufflin' up the church just like this' (here the farmer executed an imitative *pas seul*), 'sit down in his seat, and say his prayers into his box-hat same as I'm doing now.' (He took Tall Hat the Second from the table, and poured—or rather puffed—an imaginary petition into its interior.)

'Now, listen to what happened next. The very day after I'd put the last shillin' into the plate—that was three months, you must remember, after I'd bought the 'at—up comes a note from the cook at the Rectory, saying as the weekly order for butter was to be reduced from six pounds to five. "I suppose it's because Master Norman's goin' to boarding school," I says to the missis. "Not it," says she, "one mouth more or less don't make no difference in a big household like that. Besides, they're not the people to cut it fine." "I wonder what it means," I says. But I hadn't long to wait. About a fortnight later I met old Charley Shott and says to him, jokin' like, "Well, Charley, how much did you pay for your Sunday box-hat?" "Cost me nothing,' said Charley laughin'. "I've run up a little bill against his Reverence for that 'at. And, what's more, I've made him pay it! By the way," says he, "what's become o' their appetites down at the Rectory? We've just received warnin' as no more poultry'll be wanted till further orders." "I don't know," says I; but it was a lie, for it come over me in a flash what it all meant. Even then, however, I wasn't *quite* sure.

'However, it was twenty-one weeks before I got the final clearing-up. Thirty-three weeks to the very day, reckoning from the Saturday which I bought the 'at, comes another message from the Rectory: "Please send six pounds of butter as before."

'Next day I went to church as usual. No sooner did Mr Abel give out his text than I saw it all, plain as daylight. The text was something about "robbery of God". There was not a thing I've told you about the 'at that was not put into that sermon. Of course, it was roundabout—all about pearls and precious stones and such like; but it was my box-hat he was driving at all the time. It was Solomon mostly as he talked about; but I nearly jumped out of my seat when he made Solomon shake his fist at the 'Oly Temple on Mount Zion and say almost the very words as I said as I drove by the church that Saturday night. First he went for me, and then he went for Charley Shott, and I can tell you that he twisted the tails of both on us to a pretty tune! Says I to myself, "Don't I know who's put you up to preaching that sermon?" And more than seven months gone since it happened! Think of that for a memory! And she sitting in her pew with a face as smooth as a dish o' cream.

'Well, I was churchwarden that year, and of course had to take the plate round. When I comes to the Rector's pew I see Mrs Abel openin' a little purse. First she takes out a sovereign, and then a shilling, and says to me, quite clear, as she dropped 'em into the plate, "All right, Mr Church, I'll be even with you yet! And here's another two pound fifteen. You can tell Charley Shott, and Tom Henderson, and all the lot on 'em, as they've paid for their Sunday 'ats. And give 'em all my kind regards." Then she counts the money out as deliberate as if she were payin' the cook's wages, and drops it into the plate wi' a clatter as could be heard all over the church. She must ha' kep' me waitin' full two minutes, all the congregation starin' and wonderin' what was up, and me lookin' like a silly calf.

'When I come out of church my wife says to me, "Sam, what's that you and Mrs Abel was whispering about?" "You mind your own business," I says, and for the first time since we were married we was very near coming to words.'

A GRAVEDIGGER SCENE

It was Sunday evening, and the congregation had dispersed. I was making my way into the church to take a last look at a famous fourteenth-century tomb. Not a soul was visible; but the sound of a pick and the sight of fresh earth announced that the sexton was at work digging a grave. I walked to the spot. A bald head, the shining top of which was now level with the surface of the ground, raised the hope that he would prove to be a sexton of the old school. I was not disappointed.

'Good evening,' I said.

'A good evening to you, sir,' said the sexton, pausing in his work with the air of a man who welcomed an excuse to rest.

'And whose grave is that you're digging?' I asked.

'Old Sally Bloxham—mother to Tom Bloxham—him as keeps the "Spotted Pig". And a bad job for him as she's gone. If it hadn't been for old Sally he'd ha' drunk hisself to death long ago. And who may *you* be?' he asked, as though realizing that this sudden burst of confidential information was somewhat rash.

'Oh, I'm nobody in particular. Just passing through and taking a look round.'

'Ah! there's lots as comes looking round, nowadays. More than there used to be. Why, bless your life, I remember the time when you nivver seed a soul in this village except the home-dwellers. And now there's bicycles and motor cars almost every day. Most on 'em just pokes their noses round, and then off they goes. Some wants to see the tomb inside, and then there's a big stone over an old doorway at the back o' the church, what they calls " 'Arrowing o' 'Ell", though *I* don't know what it means. You've 'eard on it? Well, I suppose it's something wonderful; but *I* could nivver see no 'Arrow and no 'Ell.'

'I'll tell you what, sexton,' I said, noticing some obviously human bones in the earth at his graveside, 'this churchyard needs a bit of new ground.'

'Ye're right there,' said he, 'it's needed that a good many years. But we can't get no new ground. Old Bob Cromwell as owns the lands on that side won't sell, and Lord —— won't give, so wot are yer to do? Why, I do believe as there's hundreds and thousands of people buried in this little churchyard. It's a big parish, too, and they've been burying their dead here since nobody knows when. Bones? Why, in some parts there's almost as much bones as there is clay. Yer puts in one, and yer digs up two: that's about what it comes to. I sometimes says to my missis, "I wonder who they'll dig up to make room for me." "Yes," she says, "and I wonder who you'll be dug up to make room for." It's scandalous, that's what I says.'

'But does the law allow you to disturb these old graves?'

'It does when they're old *enough*. But you can't be over particular in a place no bigger than this. Of course, we're a bit careful like. But ask no questions, and I'll tell yer no lies.'

'But this grave you're digging now; how long is it since the last interment was made in the same ground?'

'Well, that's a pretty straight 'un. That's what I call coming to the point!—Thank 'ee sir—and good luck to you and yours!—However, since you seem a plain-dealing gentleman, I'll tell you summat as I wouldn't tell everybody. You poke your stick about in that soil over there, and you'll find some bits as belonged to Sam Wiggin's grandfather on his mother's side.' (I poked my stick as directed.) 'That's his tooth you've got now; but I won't swear to it, as things had got a bit mixed, no doubt, afore they put him in. Wait a bit, though. What's under that big lump at the end o' my spade?' (He reached out his spade and touched a clod; I turned it over and revealed the thing it hid: he examined it carefully.) 'You see, you can generally tell after a bit o' practice what belongs to what. Putting two and two together—what with them bones coming up so regular, and that bit o' coffin furniture right on the top on 'em—I reckon we've struck 'im much as he was put down in '62.'

'Are none of his relatives living?' I asked.

'Why, yes, of course they're living. Didn't I tell yer as he was grandfather to Sam Wiggin—that's 'im as farms the Leasowes at t'other end of the village. What'll he say?—why, nothing o' course. Them as sees nothing, says nothing.'

'But,' I said, 'if Sam comes to church next Sunday he'll see his grandfather's bones sticking out all over this grave.'

' 'Ow's 'e to know they're his grandfather's? There's no name on 'em,' said the sexton.

'But surely he will remember that his grandfather was buried in this spot.'

'Not 'im! 'E don't bother 'is 'ead about grandfathers. Sam Wiggin! Doesn't know 'e ever had a grandfather. Somebody else might take it up? Not in this parish. Besides, we've all got used to it. Folks here is all mixed up wi' one another while they're living, so they don't mind gettin' a bit mixeder when they're dead.'

'But is the parson used to it along with the rest of you?'

'Well, yer see, I allus clears up before he comes to bury—ribs and shins and big 'un's as won't break up. Skulls breaks up easy; you just catches them a snope with yer spade, and they splits up down the joinin'. Week afore last I dug up two beauties under that yew; anybody might a' kep' 'em for a museum. I've knowed them as would ha' done it, and sold 'em for eighteenpence apiece. But I couldn't bring my mind to it.'

'So you just broke them up, I suppose?'

'No, I didn't. One on 'em belonged to a man as I once knowed; leastways I remember him as a young chap. He was underkeeper at the Hall. The young woman he wanted to marry wouldn't 'ave 'im, so he shot hisself wi' a rook gun. I knowed it was 'im by the 'ole in 'is 'ead, no bigger nor a pea. Just think o' that! No bigger nor a big pea, I tell yer, and as round as if it had been done wi' a punch. I told my missis about it when I went 'ome to my tea. I says, "Do yer remember 'Arry Pole, the young keeper in the old lord's time, what shot hisself over that affair wi' Polly Towers?" "Remember 'im?" she says. "Why, I used to go out walking wi' 'im myself afore he took up wi' Polly." "I thought you did," I says; "well, there's 'is skull.

See that little 'ole in it, clean as if it had been cut wi' a punch? He never shot hisself, not 'e!" Why, bless yer heart, doesn't it stand to sense that if 'e'd done it 'isself, he'd a'most ha' blowed 'is 'ead off, leastways made a 'ole a lot bigger nor that? And wot's more, there'd ha' been a 'ole on the other side, and there wasn't any sign o' one.'

'But perhaps it wasn't 'Arry Pole's skull?'

'Yes, it was. Why, where's the sense of its not bein'? I remember his bein' buried as if it was yesterday, and knowed the spot quite well. And do you think it likely that two men 'ud be put in the same grave both wi' rook bullets in their 'eads? If it wasn't 'Arry Pole, who was it?'

'But wasn't all this gone into at the inquest?'

'Well, you see, it's over forty years since it 'appened; but I can remember as the 'ole were looked into, and there was a good deal o' talk at the time. There was two men as said they seed him wi' the gun in his hand, and a mournful look on his face, like. And so, what wi' one thing and another, when they couldn't find who else had killed him, they give the verdict as he must ha' killed hisself. So, you see, they made it out some'ow. But you'll never make me believe 'e did it 'isself—not after I've seen that 'ole.'

'I wonder who shot him,' I said meditatively.

'Yes, and you'll 'ave to go on wondering till the Judgment Day. You'll find out then. All I can tell yer is that it wasn't me, and it wasn't Polly Towers. However, when I found his skull I didn't break it as I do wi' most on 'em. I just kep' it in a bag and put it back when I filled in the grave.

'But you were askin' me about Parson. Well, I told him the state o' the churchyard when he come to the living. At first he took it pretty easy. "Hide 'em as far as you can, Johnny," he says to me. "And remember there's this great consolation—they'll all be sorted out on the Judgment Day."

'But one day something 'appened as give Parson a pretty start. It was one of these chaps in motors, I reckon, as did it. I see him one Saturday night rootin' about the churchyard and lookin' behind them laurels where I used to pitch all the bits and bobs of bone as I see lying about. I've often wished I'd took the number on his motor, and then we'd ha' catched him fine! But he was a gentlemanly-looking young feller, and I didn't suspect nothing at the time.

'Well, next morning, when Parson comes to read the Service, what do you think he found? Why, there was a man's thigh-bone, large as life, stuck in the middle of the big Prayer-book at the Psalms for the day. Then, when he opens the Bible to read the lessons, blessed if there wasn't a coffin-plate, worn as thin as a sheet of paper, marking the place. Then he goes into the pulpit, and the first thing he sees was a jawbone full of teeth lyin' on the cushion; there was ribs in the book-rack; there was a tooth in his glass of water, there was bones everywhere—you never see such a sight in all yer life! The young man must ha' taken a basketful into the church. Some he put into the pews, some into the collectin' boxes, some under the cushions—you never knew where you were going to find 'em next!'

'That was a blackguardly thing to do,' I said. 'The man who did it deserves the cat.'

'So he does,' said Johnny. 'But I can tell yer, it's made us more partikler ever since. Everything behind them laurel bushes was cleared out and buried next day, and, my eye, you wouldn't believe what a lot there was! Barrer-loads!

'I'm told that when Lord ——, up at the Hall, heard on it, he nearly killed hisself wi' laughin'. There's some folks'—here Johnny lowered his voice—'there's some folks *as thinks that his lordship 'ad a 'and in it hisself.* Some says it was one of them wild chaps as 'e's allus got staying with him. That's more likely, in my opinion. But it wouldn't surprise me, just between you and me, to hear some day that his lordship was going to give us a bit o' new ground.'

HOW I TRIED TO ACT THE
GOOD SAMARITAN

ONE of the chief actors in the incident about to be related was a machine, and it is important that the reader should have this machine in his mind's eye. It was a motor-bicycle, furnished in the midst with a sputtering little engine, said to contain in its entrails the power of three horses and a half. To the side thereof was attached a small vehicle like a bath-chair, in which favoured friends of the writer are from time to time either permitted or invited to ride.

On this occasion the bath-chair was empty, and a long journey was drawing to a close. It is true that at various periods of the day I had enjoyed the company of a passenger in this humble but lively little carriage. The first had been a clergyman, who, I believe, had invented a distant engagement for the sole purpose of inducing me to give him a ride in my car. To him there had succeeded a series of small boys, picked up in various villages, each of whom, at the conclusion of a brief but mad career through space, was duly dismissed with a penny and a strict injunction to be a good lad to his mother. The last lift had been given to an aged wayfarer whose weary and travel-stained appearance had excited my compassion. No sooner, however, was the machine under weigh than I discovered, in spite of my will to believe otherwise, that my passenger was suffering not from fatigue, but from intoxication. To get rid of him was no easy matter, and the employment of stratagem became necessary. What the stratagem was, I shall pass over; I will only say that it was not in accordance with any *recognized* form of the categorical imperative. However, the ruse succeeded, and now, as I have said, the car was empty. Thus were concluded the prolegomena to that great act of altruism which was to crown the day.

It was in a part of the country consecrated by the genius of a great novelist (as what part of England is not?) that these things took place. I found myself in the narrow streets of an ancient town—and it was market-day. The roadway was thronged with red-faced men and women; and flocks of sheep, herds of cattle and pigs, provided the motor-cyclist with a severe probation to the nerves. With much risk to myself, and not a little to other people, I emerged from this place of danger and joyfully swept over the bridge into the broad highway beyond the town.

Turning a corner, I became suddenly aware that the road a hundred yards ahead was again blocked. Two carriers' carts, a brewer's waggon, and some other miscellaneous vehicles were drawn up anyhow in the road, and the drivers of these, having descended from their various perches, were gathered around a figure lying prostrate on the ground. I, too, alighted and forced my way into the group. In the midst was an old man, his countenance pallid as death, save where a broad stream of blood, pouring from a gash two inches long, crimsoned his cheek from eye to chin. There was a great bruise on his temple, and again on the back of his head—for he had spun round in falling—was a lump the size of a pullet's first egg.

' 'Oss ran away and pitched him on the curb,' said one whom I questioned. 'He's dying,' said another, 'if not already dead.' For myself, I turned sick at the sight; nevertheless, I could not help being struck by the vigorous actions and attitude of an old woman, who, armed with a bucket of water and a roller towel, seemed to be not merely bathing his wounds, but giving the whole man a bath. I also noted the figure of a clergyman, of whom all that I distinctly recall is that he had a tassel round his hat.

'We must take him to the hospital,' said I. 'No,' said an elderly man; 'He'll be dead before you get him there. He's nearly gone already. Better fetch a doctor.'

'Has anybody got a bicycle?' said the clergyman in the slightly imperious accents of Keble College. 'Yes,' I replied, 'I've got one, and just the sort of bicycle for this business, too.' 'You'd better fetch Ross,' said the same voice, speaking once more in the tones which indicate conscious possession of the Last Word on Everything Whatsoever. 'No,' said the old woman, with enough defiance in her manner to frighten a Pope, 'No, Ross's no good. Fetch Conklin.' 'All right,' I said; 'if one of you will show me where Conklin lives, I'll fetch him in a brace of shakes.'

Instantly the whole company, saving only the parson and the old woman, volunteered. Selecting one who seemed of lighter weight than the rest (he was a boy), I jumped up, called to my three horses, yoked up the half-horse (kept in reserve for great occasions), and, letting all loose at once, drove at top speed in the direction of Conklin's abode.

Then was seen in the streets of that old town such a scurrying and scattering, both of men and beasts, as the world has not beheld since the most desperate moments of John Gilpin's ride. Back over the bridge, where Cavaliers and Roundheads once stood at push of pike for fifty minutes by 'the towne clocke'; through the market-place, where the cheap-jack ceased lying that he might regard us; past the policeman at the Cross (slower at this point); up the steep gradient of the High Street; right through a flock of geese (illustrious bird! who not only warnest great cities of impending ruin, but keepest thyself out of harm's way better than any four-footed beast of the field), we drove our headlong course; and, in less time than this paragraph has taken to write, I stood on the doorstep of the doctor's house. In another minute I had seen him and told my tale.

The doctor received my gushings with perfect impassivity, and responded with the merest apology for a grunt. But the repeated allusion to flowing blood seemed at last to rouse him. He seized a black bag that stood on the table, thrust in the necessary tackle, and said, 'Come along.'

In the race back to the Field of Blood, I had no leisure to analyse the structure of Conklin's mind. But a few remarks which he shouted in my ear revealed the fact that his interests were by no means confined to the performance of professional duty. I could not help wondering what Ross was like. If any reader should be taken suddenly ill while staying in that town, my advice, formed mainly on negative data, would be to send for Ross during the acute stage of the malady, and to try Conklin's treatment in convalescence. Or, better still, call them both in at once, and then take your choice.

These mental observations were scarcely completed when a turn in the road brought us in sight of our goal. Will the reader believe me when I tell him that the goal seemed to have vanished? I could scarcely believe it myself. Not a soul was to be seen. Stare as I would, no human form, living or dead, prostrate or upright, wounded or whole, answered to my gaze. Men, horses, and carts—all were gone! The whole insubstantial pageant had faded, leaving not a wrack behind.

'This is the place,' I said to Conklin; 'but the man has disappeared.' For answer, he looked fixedly into the pupil of my left eye, expecting, no doubt, to find there unmistakable signs of lunacy. 'Wait a bit,' I cried, divining his thoughts; 'here's somebody who will clear it up.' And I pointed to a cottage-door at which I suddenly espied the old woman whose handling of the roller-towel had so impressed me. 'Where,' I shouted, addressing her, 'where is the wounded man?' 'Took away,' was the laconic reply. 'Took away!' I said; 'and who has had the impudence to take him away?'

'Why,' said the old woman, 'you hadn't been gone more'n two minutes when his niece—her as keeps his house—comes driving home in a big cart. "Hello!" she says, "blest if that isn't Uncle Fred!" "Yes," says one of 'em, "and got it pretty badly this time, I can tell yer. There's a gentleman just gone to fetch Conklin." "Conklin?" says she. "I'll Conklin 'im! Who do you think's going to pay 'im? Not *me!* Let 'im as fetches 'im pay 'im. 'Ere," she says, "some of yer help to put this old man on the bottom of my cart, and look sharp, or Conklin'll be here in a minute." So they shoves the poor old thing on to the floor of the cart with a sack of 'taters to keep him steady, and Eliza—that's her name—'its the 'oss with a long stick as she carried instead of a whip, sets off at full gallop, and was out of sight almost before you could say so. Somebody else took the old man's pony, and the rest of 'em all made off as fast as they could.'

'And what did that clergyman do?' I asked.

'Jumped on his bicycle and went 'ome to his tea,' said the old woman.

'The sneak!' I cried.

'You couldn't ha' used a better word,' said the old woman, 'and there's plenty of people in this parish who'd be glad to hear you say it. And the worst of it is, there's plenty more like him!' This last was shouted with great emphasis, perhaps with a view to Conklin's edification, but at all events with the air of a person who could produce supporting evidence were such to be demanded.

There was a pause, and I endeavoured to collect my thoughts. 'Doctor,' I said, making a desperate attempt to get as near the Good Samaritan as these untoward developments rendered possible, 'Doctor, what's your fee?'

'The expression on your face is the best fee I've had for a long time,' said the doctor; 'I'm sorry I didn't bring my kodak.'

'Doctor Conklin,' I resumed, 'I'll tell you one thing. You and this old lady are the only members of the company who carry away an untarnished reputation from this episode. As for me, I have been made a perfect fool of. As for the rest of them,'—I waited for words to come, and, finally lapsing into melodrama, said—'as for the rest of them, I leave them to the company of their own consciences.'

'There's one of 'em as hasn't got any,' said the old woman.

'MACBETH' AND 'BANQUO'
ON THE BLASTED HEATH

THE scene was the top of a lofty hill in Northamptonshire, crossed by the high road to London. The time, late afternoon of a dark and thunderous day in July.

I had journeyed many miles that day—on wheels, according to the fashion of this age—and had passed and overtaken hundreds, literally hundreds, of tramps. With some of these I had already conversed as we sheltered from recurrent storms under hedges or wayside trees; and I had committed, with a joyful conscience, all the vices of indiscriminate charity.

But now the rain came on in earnest. Blacker and blacker grew the skies, and, just as I reached the top of this shelterless hill, the windows of heaven were opened, and the flood burst.

No house was in sight. But, looking round me, in that spirit of despair bred of black weather and a wet skin, I saw, in a large bare field, a shepherd's box—a thing on wheels, large enough, perhaps to accommodate a prosperous vendor of ice-cream. Abandoning my iron friend to the cold mercies of the ditch, I scaled the wall, crossed the field, and dived into the dry interior of the box. At one bound I entered into full possession of the freedom of Diogenes in his tub, with no Alexander to bother me. The absolute seclusion of the country was all my own.

The box was closed by a half-door, with an aperture above facing towards the road. Had the animal inside possessed four legs instead of two, his body would have filled the box, and his head would have projected into the rain. Though my head was inside, I could see well enough what was going on in the road. Presently there passed two cyclists—a young man and woman—racing through the storm. I shouted to them, but my voice was drowned in the din. Some minutes elapsed, during which I had the company of my thoughts. Then suddenly there appeared on the wall the incarnate figures of two tramps, un-questionably such. They had seen the box, and were making tracks for it with all their might.

I confess that for a moment my spirit quailed within me. Seen at that distance, the newcomers looked ugly customers; they had me in a trap, and, had I possessed pistols, I verily believe that I should have 'looked to the priming'. But, having no alternatives of that kind before me, necessity determined the policy I was to pursue, and I resolved at once for a friendly attitude. Waiting till the tramps were well within hearing, I thrust my head from the aforesaid aperture and cried aloud as follows:

'Walk up, gentlemen! It's my annual free day. No charge for seats.'

Macbeth and Banquo were not more affrighted by the appar-ition of witches on the blasted heath than were these two indi-viduals when they heard the voice from the box, and saw the face of him that spake. They stopped dead, stared, and, though I won't give this on oath, turned pale. I believe they were genu-inely scared.

Presently one of them—say Macbeth—broke into a loud and merry laugh. The sound of it was worth more to me at that moment than a sheaf of testimonials, for I remembered Car-lyle's dictum that there is nothing irremediably wrong with any man who can utter a hearty laugh.

'All right, guvnor,' came the reply, 'we'll take two stalls in the front row.'

'Good!' I replied. 'Wire just received from the Prince and Princess of Wales resigning their seats! Bring your own opera-glasses, and don't forget the fans.'

'Got 'em both,' said Macbeth.

A moment later I found myself in close physical proximity to two of the dirtiest rascals in Christendom. A reconciler of op-posites, bent on knocking our heads together, would have had an easy task, for there was not more than eight inches between them. Misfortunes are said to bring out the fragrance of noble natures, and I can testify that the wetting these men had received most effectually brought out the fragrance of theirs. And the ventilation was none too good.

The language in which the newcomers proceeded to introduce themselves was not of the kind usually printed, though it had a distinctly theological tinge. More strenuous blasphemy I have never heard on land—or sea.

The introductions concluded—they were sufficient—Macbeth, as though suddenly recollecting an interrupted train of thought, broke out: 'Say, mister, did yer see them two go by on bicycles just now?'

'Yes.'

'Well, I see 'em, quarter of a mile oop the road, crouching oonder t'hedge'—he spoke Yorkshire[1]—'wet to skin, and she nowt on but a cotton blouse. So I sez to her, "My dear, ye'll get yer death o' cold." "Yes," she says, "and me with a weak chest." Pore young thing, I'm fair sorry for her. I towd t'young man to tek his co-at off and put it ra-ownd her. "That'll do no good," he sez; "she's wet through a'ready." "Well," I sez "she's not been wet through all her life, has she? Why didn't you put it on her while she were dry? Sense? You've got no more sense nor a blind rabbit." But it was no good. My! What rain! Nivver see nothing like it. They'll be fair drownded. I think I'll go and fetch 'em in. Holy potatoes!' (Will anyone explain this expression? It was evoked by a crash of thunder which burst immediately above the box and seemed to hurl us into space.)

'No good fetching 'em in now,' I replied, taking a point of view which I afterwards saw to have been that of the Priest and the Levite. 'They'd suffer more damage getting here than staying where they are. Besides, where would you put 'em?'

'That's trew,' said Macbeth. 'This ain't no place for ladies, anyhow.' (It wasn't!) 'But just think of that pore young thing—nowt on, I tell yer, but a cotton blouse. Hello! there's a cart coming. I'll tell t'man to tek 'em oop.'

---

[1] The reader who would get the full flavour of Macbeth's conversation should translate it, if he can, into a broad Yorkshire dialect. This I have indicated here and there by the spelling of a word, which is as far as, or perhaps farther than, my own competence extends.

Out jumped Macbeth into the pelting rain, and presently I heard him shouting to the man in charge: 'Hey, mister! There's a young man and woman crouching under t-hedge oop t'ro-ad. She nowt on but a cotton blouse! It isn't sa-afe, yer know, in this thoonder and lightnin'. Tek her oop, and put a sack or two on her.'

I gathered the result of the interview was satisfactory to Macbeth, for presently he came back, steaming, into the box. For some minutes he continued to mutter with the thunder, about 'poor young things', 'cotton blouses', and 'weak chests'.

But the altruistic passion in the man had spent itself for the moment, and now the conversation began to take other forms. Banquo began to enter into the dialogue. His contributions so far had been mainly interjectory and blasphemous—a department of which he was obviously a more versatile exponent than the other, who was by no means a 'prentice hand. And here I must note a curious thing. Whether it was that the box afforded no proper theatre for exhibiting the natural dignity of my carriage, or that the light was not good, or that I am a ruffian at heart and had been caught at an unguarded moment—whatever the true cause may have been, I am certain that up to this moment my two companions had no suspicion that I was not a tramp like themselves.

It was Banquo who unmasked the truth. His mind was less preoccupied with the sufferings of the 'poor young thing', and no doubt had been taking observations. The result of these he proceeded to communicate to Macbeth by a series of nudges and winks which, in the close proximity of the moment, I felt rather than saw. On the whole, I am sorry that their first delusion—if, indeed, it was a delusion, of which I am genuinely doubtful—was not maintained. However, the discovery opened the way to fresh developments. They ceased to address me as 'Johnny', 'Old Joker', or something worse; ceased swearing, for which, lover of originality as I am, I was thankful; and began generally to pay me the respect due to the fact that the soles of my boots were intact. Theirs were in a very different condition.

I can't disguise that there was something like an awkward

pause. But I exerted myself to bridge the chasm, and, thanks to them rather than to me, it was bridged.

'Where are you going to-night?' I asked as soon as the *modus vivendi* was assured.

'Ain't going nowhere in particular,' said Banquo. 'We just go anywhere.'

'What!' I said, 'don't you know where you'll pass the night?'

'Well, it's just this way,' returned the other. 'Me and my mate here are musicians, and we just go this way and that according to where the publics are. It's in the publics we makes what living we gets—singing in the bars and cadging for drink and coppers.'

'And a bloomin' shame we should have to do it!' chimed in Macbeth. 'But what can yer do? My trade's a mason; Leeds is where I come from; but when they're short of work, if you've got *two* grey hairs and another chap's got only *one*, you gets the sack, and has to live as best yer can.

'God knows I don't want this beastly life. But it's a good thing I've got it to turn to. Most on 'em has nowt but their trades, and them's the ones as has to starve. But me and my mate here happens to be moosical. Used to sing in St —— Church in Leeds. Leading bass, I was—a bit irregular, I'll own, and that's why they wouldn't keep me on. My mate plays the cornet. He used to be in the band of the —— Fusiliers. Served in South Africa, he did, and got a sock in the face from a shell; yer can see the 'ole under his eye. Good thing it didn't 'it him in the ma-outh, or he wouldn't ha' been able to play the cornet any more. Know Yorkshire, mister?'

I replied that I did.

'Well, if yer knows Yorkshire, yer knows there's plenty of music up there. They can tell music, when they hear it, in Yorkshire, *that* they can! But these caownties down here, why, the people knows no more about music nor pigs. They can't tell the difference between a man what really *can* sing and one of these 'ere 'owlin' 'umbugs that goes draggin' little children up and daown t' streets. That sort makes more money than we does. And I tell you, him 'ere'—indicating Banquo—'is a good cornet player. 'Ere, Banquo, fetch it out o' your pocket, lad, and play the gentleman a toon.'

As far as I could judge, Banquo's pocket was situated somewhere in the middle of his back, for it was from a region in that quarter, where I had already felt a hard excrescence, due as I might have thought to an unextracted cannon-ball received in South Africa, that the cornet was produced.

'Play the gentleman "The Merry Widder",' said Macbeth, 'and wait till the thunder's stopped rolling before you begin.'

The 'Merry Widder' was well and duly played, and fully bore out Macbeth's eulogy of the player. It was followed by something from *Maritana*, and other things which I forget. Though the mouth of the trumpet was only a few inches from the drum of my ear, yet the din of the rain on the roof was such that the effect was not unpleasant—at all events, it was a welcome relief from the frightful strain on the olfactory organ. The man, I say, was a good player, and I remember wishing, as I listened to him, that there was anything in life that I could do half as well.

As he finished one of his selections, the gloom deepened, it became almost dark as night, the rain ceased for a moment, and there was silence; and then there shot in upon us a blast of fire and a bolt of thunder, so near and so overwhelming that I verily believe it was a narrow escape from death.

'That's something to put the fear of God into a man,' said Macbeth, as the volley rolled into distance. 'My crikey! But I've heard say, mister, that the thunder is the voice of the wrath of God.'

'I'm sure it is,' I replied.

'Sounds like it anyhow. I wonder if that there chap with the cart has got the young woman under cover. She'll be scared out of her life. Eh, but isn't it dark? It might be half-past ten. Here, matey'—to Banquo—'let's have something in keepin' loike. Give us "Lead, Kindly Light", lad, on t'cornet, and I'll sing the bass. I want t' gentleman to hear my voice.'

The hymn was sung in a voice as good as some that have made great fortunes, but with a depth of emotion which occasionally spoilt the notes; and I can say little more than that the singing, in that strange setting, with muttering thunder for an undertone, was a thing I shall not forget.

'Do you know anything about that hymn?' said Macbeth (the tears made watercourses down his dirty face) when it was over.

'Yes,' I said, 'a little.'

'But I know *all* about it,' replied Macbeth. 'Him as wrote that hymn was Cardinal Newman. They say he wrote it at sea, maybe he wrote it in a storm—like this. He was a Protestant, and was just turning into a Catholic. Didn't know whether he would or whether he wouldn't, loike. That's what he means when he says, "Lead, Kindly Light." He was i' th' dark, and wanted lightin'. It was *all* dark, don't you see, just loike it is naow.'

Some minutes elapsed, during which neither Banquo nor I said a word. I stole a glance at the ' 'ole under his eye', and saw that it was no laughing matter to 'get a sock in the face from a shell'. The human profile, on that side, had virtually disappeared; jaw and cheek-bone were smashed in; there was neither nostril nor ear; the lower eyelid was missing; the eye itself was evidently sightless, and a constant trickle of tears ran down into the hideous scar below.

I thought of this man wandering over the earth, abhorred of all beholders; I thought of the music he managed to make with the remnant of his mutilated face; I thought also of the rigour of Destiny and the kindliness of Death. I remember the words running in my head, 'He hath no form nor comeliness. Yet he was wounded for our transgressions, and the chastisement of our peace was upon him.'

I averted my glance, but not before Banquo had discovered that I was looking at him. 'Ha,' he said; 'you're lookin' at my face. It's a beauty, isn't it? They ought to put it on the board outside the recruitin' stations, as a sort of inducement to good-lookin' young men. Help to make the Army popular wi' the young women, don't you see? "George, why don't you join the Army and get a face like that? You'd be worth lookin' at then." Can't you hear 'em saying it? Oh yes, I'm proud o' my face, *that* I am! So's my old gal. That's why she left me and the kids the day I come home—never seen her since. Every time I draws my pension I says to myself, "Bill, my lad, that face o' yours is cheap at the price. Keep up your pecker, my hearty; you'll make yer fortune when Mr Barnum sees yer! It's a bloomin' good investment, that's what I calls it. Gives yer a sort o' start in life. Makes folks glad to see yer when you drops in to tea. And then I'm always feelin' as though I wanted to have my photograph taken—and that's nice, too. So you see, takin' it all round, it's quite a blessin' to have a face like mine.'

I was silent, not knowing what to say. Banquo went on:

'I thought when I come out o' the 'orspital as it were all up wi' playin' the cornet. But I made up my mind as I'd try. So I kep' up practice all the way home from the Cape, and when we got to Southampton I could just manage to blow into the mouth-piece. It hurt a bit, too, I can tell you. You see, I can only play on one side o' my mouth— like this. But I got used to it after a time; and now I can play a'most as well wi' half a mouth as I used to do wi' a whole un.'

Again I was silent, for there was a tangle of thoughts in my mind, and behind it all a vague, uncomfortable sense that I was come to judgment. From this sprang a sudden resolve to change the subject, which was unpleasant to me in more senses than one. So I said, after the pause, 'What about your pension?'

'Pension, did you say? Well, you see, sir, I've been in a bit o' trouble since I come home. There was a kind old gent as give me three months in the choke-hole for not behavin' quite as handsome as I ought to. "It'll spile all my good looks, your Worship," I says when he sentenced me. "Remove the prisoner, officer!" he says; and I thinks to myself, "I'd like to remove *you,* old gentleman, and see what you'd look like on a hammynition waggon, wi' two dead pals under your nose, and a pom-pom shell a-burstin' in your ear-'ole." But I've had one good friend, anyhow; and I don't want a better—and that's him there' (indicating Macbeth). 'He's a *man,* he is! I can tell you one thing—if it hadn't been for him there, I'd ha' sent the other half o' my head to look for the first half long ago—and that's the truth!'

While this conversation was proceeding Macbeth, *more suo,*

continued to mutter like a man in a troubled dream, now humming a bar of the tune, now drawling out a phrase from the words, 'O'er moor and fen, o'er crag and torrent, till the night is gone'—this, I believe, he repeated several times, lighting his pipe in the intervals and spitting out of the door. Then he went on more articulately: 'Rum go, ain't it—me singing that hymn in a place like this? Sung it in church 'undreds o' times. We give it sometimes in the streets. It's part of our *répertoire*' (he pronounced this word quite correctly). 'But I can't help makin' a babby o' mysen whenever I think o' what it means. I don't think of it, as a rewle. I should break down if I did; like as I nearly did just naow. Oh Lor'! I can get on all right till I comes to th' end. It's them "angel faces" wot knocks the stuffing out o' *me*!'

'Same 'ere,' I replied; and I put my head out of the aperture for a breath of fresh air.

> 'When shall we three meet again
> In thunder, lightning, or in rain?'